HONEYMOON SUITE

by Richard Bean

English Touring Theatre

English Touring Theatre was set up eleven years ago with the aim of bringing quality theatre to as many people as possible throughout the country.

In our first eleven years we have toured over thirty productions, and gained a reputation for work which is carefully conceived, true to the play and respects its audience. We have won eighteen major awards, taken eleven productions into London, and worked with some of the most talented and respected artists in the country.

Most of our work has been classical revivals. Our successes include Alan Cumming's *Hamlet*, Kelly Hunter in *As You Like It*, our award winning production of *Hedda Gabler* with Alexandra Gilbreath, both parts of Shakespeare's *Henry IV*, Timothy West and Emma Cunniffe in *The Master Builder*, Diana Quick and Daniel Evans in *Ghosts* and Timothy West in *King Lear*, which was a tremendous hit at The Old Vic. We also enjoyed considerable success with the world premières of Jonathan Harvey's *Rupert Street Lonely Hearts Club* and *Hushabye Mountain*, and our production of Peter Gill's award winning *The York Realist* enjoyed a sold out run at the Royal Court and transferred to the West End.

At the heart of everything we do is the passionately held belief that quality theatre does not have to be elitist, and that people everywhere expect and deserve the best. We are committed to making our work as accessible as possible, and this is why in addition to the work on stage we also provide a first class Education Programme to accompany our tours.

We are constantly looking to find new supporters of our work, and our Members' Scheme and Supporters' Circles enable our audience to help us continue to tour high quality productions throughout the country.

Stephen Unwin
Artistic Director

Tim Highman
Executive Director

Awards

In its first eleven years English Touring Theatre has won eighteen major awards:

SHAKESPEARE'S GLOBE SAM WANAMAKER AWARD
Stephen Unwin

CRITICS' CIRCLE AWARD
BEST PLAY *The York Realist*

SUNDAY TIMES IAN CHARLESON AWARDS
FIRST PRIZE Mark Bazeley *The Seagull*
FIRST PRIZE Alexandra Gilbreath *Hedda Gabler*
SECOND PRIZE Daniel Evans *Ghosts*

TMA AWARDS
BEST ACTOR Timothy West *King Lear*
BEST ACTRESS Diana Quick *Ghosts*
BEST ACTRESS IN A SUPPORTING ROLE Emma Cunniffe *The Master Builder*
BEST TOURING PRODUCTION *Hedda Gabler*
BEST ACTRESS Kelly Hunter *As You Like It*
BEST ACTOR Alan Cumming *Hamlet*

MANCHESTER EVENING NEWS AWARDS
BEST ACTOR IN A VISITING PRODUCTION Timothy West *King Lear*
BEST ACTRESS IN A VISITING PRODUCTION Diana Quick *Ghosts*
BEST ACTOR IN A VISITING PRODUCTION Timothy West *The Master Builder*
BEST NEW PLAY *Rupert Street Lonely Hearts Club*
BEST ACTOR Bette Bourne *The Importance of Being Earnest*

WHATSONSTAGE.COM AWARD
BEST SUPPORTING ACTOR Richard Coyle *The York Realist*

CITY LIFE AWARD
BEST PLAY *Rupert Street Lonely Hearts Club*

Cast

In alphabetical order

WHITCHELL	John Alderton
IRENE	Sara Beharrell
EDDIE	Liam Garrigan
IZZY	Caroline O'Neill
TITS	Jeremy Swift
MARFLEET	Marjorie Yates

Honeymoon Suite
received its first
performance
on 8 January 2004
at the Royal Court.

Creative & Production Team

Creative Team

WRITER	Richard Bean
DIRECTOR	Paul Miller
DESIGNER	Hayden Griffin
LIGHTING DESIGNER	Andy Phillips
ORIGINAL MUSIC	Terry Davies
ASSISTANT DESIGNER	Riette Hayes-Davies
CASTING DIRECTOR	Simone Reynolds
ASSOCIATE DESIGNER FOR ETT	Sara Perks

Production Team

HEAD OF PRODUCTION	Simon Curtis
COSTUME SUPERVISOR	Chris Cahill
TECHNICAL MANAGER	Rupert Barth von Wehrenalp
COMPANY STAGE MANAGER	Abi Duddleston
DEPUTY STAGE MANAGER	Clare Loxley
ASSISTANT STAGE MANAGER	Amy Almond
TECHNICAL STAGE MANAGER	Darren Joyce
SOUND TECHNICIAN	Jaime Leonard

Cast Biographies

John Alderton
WHITCHELL

Theatre includes: *What the Butler Saw* and *Waiting for Godot* at RNT; *Spring and Port Wine* at Apollo Theatre; *Dutch Uncle* at Aldwych Theatre; *The Night I Chased the Woman with an Eel*, *Judies*, *The Birthday Party*, *Confusions*, *Rattle of a Simple Man* and *Casebook* at Savoy Theatre; *Haven't We Met Somewhere Before?* at Young Vic; *Special Occasions* and *See How They Run* at Theatre of Comedy; *The Maintenance Man* at Thorndike Theatre; *Loot* at West Yorkshire Playhouse.

Television includes: *He Knew He Was Right*; *Down to Earth*; *Mrs Bradley Mysteries*; *Heartbeat*; *Tonight at 8.30*; *Keeping Tom Nice*; *Forever Green*; *The Rivals*; *Macbeth*; *Father's Day*; *Trelawney of 'The Wells'*; *Please Sir*; *My Wife Next Door*; *Upstairs, Downstairs*; *No Honestly*.

Film: *Calendar Girls*; *Mrs Caldicot's Cabbage Wars*; *Clockwork Mice*; *Duffy*; *Please Sir*; *Zardoz*; *It Shouldn't Happen to a Vet*.

Sara Beharrell
IRENE

Trained at Guildhall School of Music and Drama.

Theatre: *Speaking Shakespeare* (platform) at RNT; *Elephant* for Filter Theatre at BAC.

Television and Film: *He Knew He Was Right*; *London's Burning*.

Liam Garrigan
EDDIE

Trained at Guildhall School of Music and Drama.

Theatre: *Gizmo* for Northern Theatre Company at RNT.

Television: *Holby City*; *Sons, Daughters and Lovers*.

Caroline O'Neill
IZZY

For ETT: *The York Realist*.

Theatre: *A Day in Dull Armour*, *One More Wasted Year* and *Stranger's House* at the Royal Court; *Vertigo* at Theatre Royal; *The Ladies of the Corridor* at Finborough Theatre; *Moses, Napoleon and the Queen* and *Increased Difficulty of Concentration* at Old Red Lion Theatre Club; *Watch Out for Mr Stork* at Regent's Park Open Air Theatre; *The Lion, the Witch and the Wardrobe* at Mermaid Theatre; *And His Name Was Jim* at Grove Theatre; *Blithe Spirit* at Dundee Rep; *Soap Box* at Forum Theatre, Manchester; *Hindle Wakes* at Library Theatre, Manchester; *The Importance of Being Earnest* at Plymouth Theatre.

Television: *Fat Friends*; *The Last Detective*; *Nurses*; *Hear the Silence*; *Wire in the Blood*; *Cutting It*; *Paradise Reclaimed*; *Behind Closed Doors*; *Doctors*; *Eastenders*; *Always & Everyone*; *Stretford Wives*; *Waking the Dead*; *Peak Practice*; *Coronation Street*; *Blood Strangers*; *Holby City*; *Hollyoaks*; *Where the Heart is*; *Queer as Folk*; *Wing and a Prayer*; *Birds of a Feather*; *Cops*; *Maisie Raine*; *The Bill*; *Out of Line*; *Shine on Harvey Moon*; *Landmarks*; *Here Comes the Mirror Man*; *The Detectives*; *Body & Soul*; *Heartbeat*; *Dead Romantics*; *The Secret*; *Coasting*; *Grange Hill*; *Coronation Street*; *Assert Yourself*.

Film: *This Little Life*.

Cast Biographies

Jeremy Swift
TITS

For ETT: *A Midsummer Night's Dream*.

Theatre: *Abigail's Party* at Hampstead Theatre and New Ambassadors Theatre; *Feel Good* for Out of Joint at Hampstead Theatre; *The Slight Witch* at Birmingham Rep and NT Studio; *Three Sisters* for Out of Joint; *What the Butler Saw*, *Devil's Disciple*, *Mother Courage* and *Peer Gynt* at RNT; *Battle of a Simple Man* at Southwold Theatre; *Trilby & Svengali* and *Heartbreak House* for Shared Experience; *Noon Day Demons* for Man in the Moon; *Gulliver's Travels* and *Bow Down* at NT Studio; *Woyzeck* at Everyman Theatre, Cheltenham; *Three Sisters* and *Cider with Rosie* at Greenwich Theatre; *No 91 - A Romance* on tour and at Almeida Theatre; *Macbeth* and *A Midsummer Night's Dream* at Haymarket Theatre, Leicester; *Measure for Measure* for The Kick Theatre; *Comedy Revue* for Stirabout Theatre.

Television: *The Alan Clark Diaries*; *Nighty Night*; *Reversals*; *Bertie and Elizabeth*; *Barbara*; *Put Out More Fags*; *The Thing About Vince*; *Bostock's Cup*; *A Christmas Carol*; *The S Club*; *Vanity Fair*; *Roger Roger*; *The Grand*; *Blind Men*; *The Student Prince*; *Pirates*; *Next of Kin*; *Dalziel & Pascoe*; *An Actor's Life for Me*; *The Paul Merton Show*.

Film: *To Kill a King*; *Gosford Park*; *The Affair of the Necklace*; *Dark Blue World*; *Mr Love*.

Marjorie Yates
MARFLEET

For ETT: *Romeo and Juliet*.

Theatre includes: *The Daughter-in-Law*, *All My Sons* and *The Price* at Young Vic; *An Inspector Calls* at Garrick Theatre; *Electra* at Donmar Warehouse; *Death of a Salesman* and *Stages* at RNT; *Richard II*, *Richard III*, *The Master Builder* and *The Plain Dealer* for RSC; *The Glass Menagerie* at Bristol Old Vic; *Small Change* and *Touched* at the Royal Court.

Television includes: *Shameless*; *A Very British Coup*; *Kisses At Fifty*.

Film includes: *The Long Day Closes*.

Creative Biographies

Richard Bean
WRITER

Theatre: *Smack Family Robinson* at Newcastle Live!; *Under the Whaleback* at the Royal Court; *The Mentalists* in the Transformation Season at NT Loft; *Mr England* at Crucible Theatre, Sheffield; *Toast* for the Royal Court at New Ambassadors Theatre.

Radio: *Unsinkable* for BBC Radio 3 as part of The Wire series; *Robin Hood's Revenge* for BBC Radio 4; *Of Rats and Men* as a Monday Night Play for BBC Radio 4. Richard was also one of the writer/performers on *Control Group Six* for BBC Radio 4.

Richard's work has won many awards and nominations. He was a winner of the Pearson New Play of the Year Award for *Honeymoon Suite* and of the George Devine Award for *Under the Whaleback*. His work on *Control Group Six* was nominated for a Writers' Guild Award and both *Unsinkable* and *Of Rats and Men* were nominated for Sony Awards.

Paul Miller
DIRECTOR

Paul Miller was Resident Director of the NT's Loft Theatre and is currently Acting Head of the National Theatre Studio.

For ETT: *Hushabye Mountain*.

Theatre includes: *Fragile Land* by Tanika Gupta at Hampstead Theatre; *The Associate* by Simon Bent at NT Loft and on tour; *Mean Tears* by Peter Gill at Sheffield Crucible Studio; *Four Nights in Knaresborough* by Paul Webb on national tour; *Tragedy: A Tragedy* by Will Eno at Gate Theatre; *Accomplices* by Simon Bent and *Mr England* by Richard Bean at NT Studio and Crucible Theatre, Sheffield; *A Penny for a Song* by John Whiting for OSC and at Whitehall Theatre; *Seascape with Sharks and Dancer* by Don Nigro and *Rosmersholm* by Ibsen at Southwark Playhouse; *The Robbers* by Schiller at Latchmere Theatre; *Sugar Sugar, Goldhawk Road* and *Bad Company* by Simon Bent at Bush Theatre.

Radio: *Unsinkable* by Richard Bean for BBC Radio 3; *The Weekend Starts Here* for BBC Radio 4; *Ladies of Letters.com* by Carole Hayman and Lou Wakefield for BBC Radio 4.

Hayden Griffin
DESIGNER

Hayden Griffin's British theatre career spans 30 years and includes 36 world première productions with writers and directors such as David Hare (including *Plenty*, *A Map of the World* and *Pravda*), David Mamet (*Glengarry Glen Ross*), Edward Bond (including *Summer*), Howard Brenton, William Gaskill and Bill Bryden for RNT, RSC, the Royal Court and many West End theatres. Hayden has designed opera and ballet for major world centres including the Royal Opera House, ENO and Birmingham Royal Ballet, collaborating with David Bintley (including *Still Life at the Penguin Café*), Guillini and Bernard Haitink (*Parsifal*). He has worked extensively around the world including New York, Los Angeles, Australia, Yugoslavia, Canada, Germany, Holland and Italy.

Hayden's feature film design credits include *Wetherby*, written and directed by David Hare, and *Intimacy*, directed by Patrice Chereau (both films won the Golden Bear Award for Best Film in Berlin).

Creative Biographies

Andy Phillips
LIGHTING DESIGNER

Andy Phillips served as resident Lighting Designer at the Royal Court from 1965 to 1972, where he designed over 80 consecutive productions, most of them world premières. Since then, he has worked extensively around the world.

Theatre and Opera includes: *Equus, Iceman Cometh, Golden Boy, Glengarry Glenross* and *Galileo* at RNT; *Equus* and *M. Butterfly* on Broadway; *California Dog Fight* and *Rat in the Skull* off Broadway; *New England, A Patriot For Me* and *Son of Man* for RSC; *Voysey Inheritance* and *Armstrong's Last Goodnight* at the Edinburgh Festival; *Waiting for Godot* for First Druid Company in Galway; *Whistle in the Dark* at Abbey Theatre, Dublin; *Forza Del Destino* at the Paris Opera; *Julius Caesar* and *Creon* at Leicester (and on tour in India); *A Street Car Named Desire* and *Sweeney Todd* in Newcastle; *Losing Time* in Hamburg; *Henceforward* in Berlin; *Job* for San Francisco Ballet; *A Month in the Country* at Albery Theatre; *The Barber of Seville* and *Way Up Stream* at Crucible Theatre, Sheffield; *Uncle Vanya* at Chichester Festival Theatre and Albery Theatre; *In The Company of Men* for RSC at Pit Theatre; *Much Ado About Nothing, Juno and the Paycock, Mother Courage and Her Children, Macbeth* and *The Anatomist* at Royal Lyceum Theatre; *Charlie's Aunt* at Crucible Theatre, Sheffield; *A Penny for a Song* for OSC. He recently designed *The Playboy of the Western World* in Stockholm.

Andy has received two Tony nominations for the Broadway productions of *Equus* (1974) and M. *Butterfly* (1989).

Terry Davies
ORIGINAL MUSIC

For ETT: *The York Realist; Hushabye Mountain; The School for Scandal*.

Theatre: *The Merry Wives of Windsor, Alice in Wonderland, A Patriot for Me, New England* and *Coriolanus* for RSC; *Scenes from the Big Picture, Luther, The Rise and Fall of Little Voice, The Misanthrope, Neaptide, The Festival of New Plays, Antigone* and *Tales from Hollywood* for RNT; *The Two Gentlemen of Verona, As You Like It, Romeo and Juliet, Love's Labour's Lost, Much Ado about Nothing, A Midsummer Night's Dream* and *Twelfth Night* for Regent's Park Open Air Theatre; *Speed-the-Plow* at Duke of York's Theatre; *Alarms and Excursions* at Gielgud Theatre; *Tongue of a Bird* at Almeida Theatre; *Sexual Perversity in Chicago* at Comedy Theatre; *Life after George* at Duchess Theatre.

Dance: *Play Without Words, The Car Man*.

Film: As Orchestrator/ Conductor: 20 films including *The Lawless Heart, The House of Mirth, The Parole Officer, A Midsummer Night's Dream* and *Shakespeare in Love*.

Terry won an Olivier Award in 2003 for *Play Without Words* and a BAFTA nomination in 2002 for *Tipping the Velvet*.

Riette Hayes-Davies
ASSISTANT DESIGNER

Theatre: As Designer: *Napoleon Noir* in London; *Murder in the Red Barn* in Frankfurt; *Rodelinda* at Aldeburgh Festival; As Design Associate: *Phantom of the Opera* in Stuttgart, Madrid and Copenhagen; *Andrea Chenier* in Sweden; As Design Assistant: *Aspects of Love* in London and New York; *Dance of the Vampires* in Vienna, Stuttgart and Hamburg; *The Mysteries* at RNT; *Titanic* in New York and on tour; *Macbeth* in Stratford and at Barbican Theatre.

Opera and Ballet: *Don Giovanni*, *Boris Godunov* and *La Traviata* at Royal Opera House; *Mahagonny* in Florence and Bastille; *Cunning Little Vixen* in Paris; *Nutcracker Suite* for English National Ballet.

Television: As Designer: *Juice*.

Film: As Production Designer: *South London Getaway*; As Art Director: *Beyond Bedlam*; As Assistant Art Director: *Nouvelle France* and *Leon the Pig Farmer*; As Design Assistant: *Out on a Limb*.

Simone Reynolds
CASTING DIRECTOR

Simone Reynolds began her career at the Royal Court where she worked for such distinguished directors as Lindsay Anderson, Max Stafford Clark and Peter Gill and writers such as Samuel Beckett, David Hare and John Osborne.

Theatre: *Mean Tears*, *Kick for Touch* and *Small Change* at Sheffield Theatres; *Shirley Valentine* at Vaudeville Theatre; *The Lady from the Sea* at Citizens' Theatre, Glasgow; *York Mystery Plays* at York Festival 1988; *Holiday* at The Old Vic; *The Overgrown Path* at the Royal Court; *Hamlet* and *Steaming* at Theatre Royal, Stratford East; *Measure for Measure* at Riverside Studios.

Television: *An Inspector Calls* (nominated for RTS Award); *Turning Points: Emma's Story* (won RTS and BAFTA Awards); *The Bill*; *Ruth Rendell: The Fallen Curtain*; *Mirad: A Boy from Bosnia*; *Grange Hill*; *The Canterville Ghost*; *The Infiltrator*; *The Politician's Wife* (won Emmy and BAFTA Awards); *The Vicar of Dibley*; *Stick With Me Kid*; *Highlander*; *Mrs 'Arris goes to Paris*; *Natural Lies*; *Thatcher - The Final Days*; *Murder East, Murder West*; *Valentine Falls*; *Saracen*; *This is David Lander*; *The Firm* (won Prix Europa in Barcelona); *Didn't you Kill my Brother*; *Up Line*; *The Young Visitors*; *The House*; *Dr Fischer of Geneva*; *Arthur's*

Hallowed Ground; *To the Lighthouse* (Rosemary Harris won Best Performance Award at Locarno Film Festival); *Daughters of Albion*.

Film: *Quicksand*; *Jinnah*; *Hanu: The Monkey Who Knew Too Much*; *Snow White, A Tale of Terror*; *Jack and Sarah*; *Matinee*; *Barcelona*; *A Business Affair*; *Voyage*; *Shining Through*; *We Think The World of You*; *The Belly of an Architect*; *White City*; *Lamb*; *Wings of Death*; *The Assam Garden*; *1919*; *Those Glory, Glory Days*; *Forever Young*; *Give my Regards to Broad Street*; *Angel*; *Ascendancy* (won Golden Bear Award in Berlin); *Brimstone and Treacle*; *Remembrance* (won First Prize at Taormina Film Festival); *Memoirs of a Survivor*; *Chariots of Fire* (won 4 Academy Awards); *The Long Good Friday*.

Creative Biographies

Sara Perks
ASSOCIATE DESIGNER
FOR ETT

Trained at Bristol Old Vic
Theatre School and
University of Kent.

For English Touring Theatre:
As Designer: *Romeo and
Juliet*; As Associate Designer:
King Lear (also The Old Vic),
John Gabriel Borkman; As
Props Buyer: *Ghosts*, *The York
Realist*, *The Caretaker*, *Love's
Labour's Lost*, *The Cherry
Orchard*, *The Master Builder*.

Theatre includes: *Habeas
Corpus* and *Romeo and Juliet*
at Northcott Theatre, Exeter;
Private Lives and *Caucasian
Chalk Circle* at Mercury
Theatre, Colchester; *Reunion*
and *Dark Pony* at King's Head
Theatre; *Aeroplane Bones* at
Bristol Old Vic; *Skylight* at
Dukes, Lancaster; *Belle* at
Gate Theatre; *Frankie &
Tommy* at Lyric Theatre
Hammersmith; *The Owl and
the Pussycat* at Redgrave
Theatre, Bristol; *Union Street*
at Plymouth Theatre Royal;
Gringos at BAC and Bristol
Old Vic; *The Old Curiosity
Shop* at Southwark
Playhouse; *The Lost Domain*
at Drum Theatre, Plymouth;
and the original Edinburgh
and London club productions
of the cult musical *Saucy Jack
and the Space Vixens*; Design
Assistant for *Carmen* at
Glyndebourne; *Rigoletto*
at Covent Garden; *Alcina*
for ENO.

Awards: The John Elvery
Theatre Design Award and a
BBC Vision Design Award for
A Midsummer Night's Dream
at Redgrave Theatre, Bristol.

Sara's future designs
include: *Macbeth* at Mercury
Theatre, Colchester; Steven
Berkoff's *The Trial* for RADA;
Si J'Etais Roi for Opera
Omnibus.

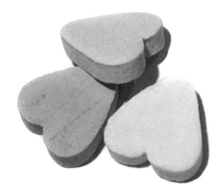

THE YORK REALIST by Peter Gill
(2001, also Royal Court and Strand Theatre, 2002)
'The best new play of the year. Wonderfully funny, engrossing theatre, sensationally performed' MAIL ON SUNDAY
CRITICS' CIRCLE AWARD FOR BEST PLAY

HUSHABYE MOUNTAIN by Jonathan Harvey
(1999, also Hampstead Theatre)
'What lifts Harvey above the ruck is his sheer heart as a writer, and his engaging wit' DAILY TELEGRAPH
CITY LIFE AWARD FOR BEST PLAY
MANCHESTER EVENING NEWS AWARD FOR BEST NEW PLAY

A DIFFICULT AGE by Marty Cruickshank (1998)
'Stephen Unwin's production has a delicate Chekhovian beauty'
THE GUARDIAN

SHELLFISH by Judith Johnson (1998)
'Shellfish is written with Johnson's starkly Scouse wit, and Pat is an utterly believable portayal of a woman making her last grab at happiness' THE GUARDIAN

RUPERT STREET LONELY HEARTS CLUB by Jonathan Harvey
(1995, also Donmar Warehouse and Criterion Theatre)
'One of the most gut-wrenching love scenes between two men ever put on stage... superb production... funny and affecting... outstanding performances' THE INDEPENDENT

Photo: Ivan Kyncl

Caroline O'Neill, Anne Reid, Ian Mercer and Lloyd Owen - *The York Realist*

Theatre for everyone

An Open Door

English Touring Theatre believes quality productions of great drama should be open to all. At the heart of everything we do is our commitment to national touring.

- We believe there should be no contradiction between artistic integrity and public accessibility, and we aim to produce work which is clear and true to the play.

- Although we have no direct control over ticket prices, we try to encourage the venues to address this issue as creatively as possible.

- Our education initiatives have earned a national reputation for creative and innovative work involving thousands of young people each year.

- We run a nationwide programme of special events and training courses hosted by established arts professionals.

- We regularly organise pre show talks, post show discussions and workshops which allow members of our audience to gain a deeper insight into the artistic process.

- We provide masterclasses and practical sessions for adults, examining all aspects of language, dramaturgy, historical context and professional theatre practice.

Access For All

English Touring Theatre regularly offers events and performances specially designed for visually and hearing impaired audience members. In collaboration with organisations such as Signing People, SPIT, STAGETEXT, Minds Eye and Vocaleyes we provide:

- BSL Interpreted, Captioned and Audio Described performances and events led by qualified professionals.

- Touch Tours providing an audio described introduction to characters, set, costumes and props, followed by a guided tour of the stage where participants are able to touch and feel materials used to create the world of the play.

Supporting excellence

'English Touring Theatre is worth its weight in gold'
THE GUARDIAN

Every year, ETT faces financial challenges and we need to raise a substantial amount of money to sustain our work. We appeal to you, our audience, to help us continue to mount productions of outstanding quality and tour them throughout the country.

There are various ways that you can help:

Member
As a Member you will receive our newsletter (Up To Date) and other benefits in return for an annual donation.

Associate Members £10 single / £15 joint
Members £30 single / £45 joint

Supporter
In joining one of our Supporters' Circles you will receive the same benefits as Members, and additional benefits including acknowledgement in our programmes. You decide how much you want to give, and you can help us even more by using the Gift Aid scheme.

Actors' Circle Minimum annual gift £75
Designers' Circle Minimum annual gift £150
Directors' Circle Minimum annual gift £1000

Shakespeare Circle Minimum one-off gift £100

For a leaflet or for further information about becoming a **Member** or joining the **Supporters' Circles**, please contact Robert Moffat, Head of Development.

Some of the people who have helped us so far are:

Alan Ayckbourn	Sam Mendes	Tom Stoppard
Roger & Sue Crowther	Stephen Mulrine	Emma Thompson
Marcia Gresham	Trevor Nunn	Monica & Peter Unwin
Sheila Hancock	Greg Parston	Paul & Kate Unwin
David Hare	Dan Persaud	Victoria Wardle
Anne & Brian Highman	Peters, Fraser & Dunlop	David Webber
Lew Hodges	Prunella Scales	Timothy West
Neil Hunter	Inka Steven	Penelope Wilton

Business supporters We also have a range of opportunities for business. Please contact Robert Moffat for full details.

Robert Moffat, Head of Development
English Touring Theatre, 25 Short Street, London SE1 8LJ
020 7450 1990 robertm@englishtouringtheatre.co.uk

English Touring Theatre

English Touring Theatre
25 Short Street, London SE1 8LJ
Tel 020 7450 1990
Fax 020 7450 1991
Minicom 020 7450 1997
email admin@englishtouringtheatre.co.uk
website www.englishtouringtheatre.co.uk

THE ENGLISH STAGE COMPANY
AT THE ROYAL COURT

The English Stage Company at the Royal Court opened in 1956 as a subsidised theatre producing new British plays, international plays and some classical revivals.

The first artistic director George Devine aimed to create a writers' theatre, 'a place where the dramatist is acknowledged as the fundamental creative force in the theatre and where the play is more important than the actors, the director, the designer'. The urgent need was to find a contemporary style in which the play, the acting, direction and design are all combined. He believed that 'the battle will be a long one to continue to create the right conditions for writers to work in'.

Devine aimed to discover 'hard-hitting, uncompromising writers whose plays are stimulating, provocative and exciting'. The Royal Court production of John Osborne's Look Back in Anger in May 1956 is now seen as the decisive starting point of modern British drama and the policy created a new generation of British playwrights. The first wave included John Osborne, Arnold Wesker, John Arden, Ann Jellicoe, N F Simpson and Edward Bond. Early seasons included new international plays by Bertolt Brecht, Eugène Ionesco, Samuel Beckett, Jean-Paul Sartre and Marguerite Duras.

The theatre started with the 400-seat proscenium arch Theatre Downstairs, and then in 1969 opened a second theatre, the 60-seat studio Theatre Upstairs. Some productions transfer to the West End, such as Terry Johnson's Hitchcock Blonde, Conor McPherson's The Weir, Kevin Elyot's Mouth to Mouth and My Night With Reg. The Royal Court also co-produces plays which have transferred to the West End or toured internationally, such as Sebastian Barry's The Steward of Christendom and Mark Ravenhill's Shopping and Fucking (with Out of Joint), Martin McDonagh's The Beauty Queen Of Leenane (with Druid Theatre Company), Ayub Khan-Din's East is East (with Tamasha Theatre Company, and now a film).

Since 1994 the Royal Court's artistic policy has again been vigorously directed to finding and producing a new generation of playwrights. The writers include Joe Penhall, Rebecca Prichard, Michael Wynne, Nick Grosso, Judy Upton, Meredith Oakes, Sarah Kane, Anthony Neilson, Judith Johnson, James Stock, Jez Butterworth, Marina Carr, Phyllis Nagy, Simon Block, Martin McDonagh, Mark Ravenhill, Ayub Khan-Din, Tamantha Hammerschlag, Jess Walters, Ché Walker, Conor McPherson, Simon Stephens, Richard Bean, Roy Williams, Gary Mitchell, Mick Mahoney, Rebecca Gilman, Christopher Shinn, Kia Corthron, David Gieselmann, Marius von Mayenburg, David Eldridge, Leo Butler, Zinnie Harris, Grae Cleugh,

Roland Schimmelpfennig, DeObia Oparei, Vassily Sigarev, the Presnyakov Brothers and Lucy Prebble. This expanded programme of new plays has been made possible through the support of A.S.K Theater Projects and the Skirball Foundation, the Jerwood Charitable Foundation, the American Friends of the Royal Court Theatre and many in association with the Royal National Theatre Studio.

In recent years there have been record-breaking productions at the box office, with capacity houses for Roy Williams' Fallout, Terry Johnson's Hitchcock Blonde, Caryl Churchill's A Number, Jez Butterworth's The Night Heron, Rebecca Gilman's Boy Gets Girl, Kevin Elyot's Mouth to Mouth, David Hare's My Zinc Bed and Conor McPherson's The Weir, which transferred to the West End in October 1998 and ran for nearly two years at the Duke of York's Theatre.

The newly refurbished theatre in Sloane Square opened in February 2000, with a policy still inspired by the first artistic director George Devine. The Royal Court is an international theatre for new plays and new playwrights, and the work shapes contemporary drama in Britain and overseas.

RECENT AWARDS FOR
THE ROYAL COURT

David Eldridge's Under the Blue Sky won the Time Out Live Award 2001 for Best New Play in the West End. Leo Butler won the George Devine Award 2001 for Most Promising Playwright for Redundant. Roy Williams won the Evening Standard's Charles Wintour Award 2001 for Most Promising Playwright for Clubland. Grae Cleugh won the 2001 Olivier Award for Most Promising Playwright for Fucking Games.

Richard Bean was joint winner of the George Devine Award 2002 for Most Promising Playwright for Under the Whaleback. Caryl Churchill won the 2002 Evening Standard Award for Best New Play for A Number. Vassily Sigarev won the 2002 Evening Standard Charles Wintour Award for Most Promising Playwright for Plasticine. Ian MacNeil won the 2002 Evening Standard Award for Best Design for A Number and Plasticine. Peter Gill won the 2002 Critics' Circle Award for Best New Play for The York Realist (English Touring Theatre). Ché Walker won the 2003 George Devine Award for Most Promising Playwright for Flesh Wound. Sandy McDade won the 2003 Evening Standard Award for Best Actress for Iron (Traverse Theatre Company). Tom Hardy won the 2003 Evening Standard Award for Outstanding Newcomer for Blood.

ROYAL COURT PROGRAMME SUPPORTERS

The Royal Court (English Stage Company Ltd) receives its principal funding from London Arts. It is also supported financially by a wide range of private companies and public bodies and earns the remainder of its income from the box office and its own trading activities.

The Royal Borough of Kensington & Chelsea gives an annual grant to the Royal Court Young Writers' Programme.

The Jerwood Charitable Foundation continues to support new plays by new playwrights through the Jerwood New Playwrights series. Since 1993 A.S.K. Theater Projects and the Skirball Foundation have funded a Playwrights' Programme at the theatre. Bloomberg Mondays, the Royal Court's reduced price ticket scheme, is supported by Bloomberg. Over the past seven years the BBC has supported the Gerald Chapman Fund for directors.

The Genesis Foundation generously supports both the International Season and the Young Writers Festival.

HONEYMOON SUITE

First published in this version in 2003 by Oberon Books Ltd.
(incorporating Absolute Classics)
521 Caledonian Road, London N7 9RH
Tel: 020 7607 3637 / Fax: 020 7607 3629

e-mail: oberon.books@btinternet.com
www.oberonbooks.com

A catalogue record for this book is available from the
British Library.

ISBN: 1 84002 406 2

Printed in Great Britain by Antony Rowe Ltd, Chippenham.

Cast in order of appearance

WHITCHELL
67 years old

EDDIE
18 years old

IRENE
18 years old

TITS
43 years old

IZZY
43 years old

MARFLEET
67 years old

All that matters is love and work.

Sigmund Freud

2004. The honeymoon suite of a seaside hotel. Against the wall, stage left, is a large and elaborate French antique double bed. A chandelier with tears of glass hangs from an ornate ceiling rose. In the back wall a door, stage right, leads into an en-suite toilet and bathroom. Down stage left is a cupboard door set in the wall. Upstage left is a door into the corridor. Downstage right is a balcony with a sea view.

WHITCHELL enters. He is a man of 67. He is wearing an old and dirty car coat, old flip flops, and an embroidered fez-like hat. His glasses have one cracked lens. His trousers are of a baggy white Indian cotton style. He carries an old and grubby supermarket carrier bag, some flowers (no wrapping paper) and a bag of shopping in a new Safeways carrier bag. He unlocks the cupboard door. He takes a champagne bucket and glasses and puts them on the bedside table. From the shopping he takes a packet of ice and fills the bucket. From the inside of his shirt he takes a bottle of champagne, picks the price label off it and puts it on ice. From the other side of his shirt he takes a packet of Cherry Bakewell cakes and puts them in the cupboard. From under his hat he takes a packet of After Eight mints. He takes a vase from the cupboard and fills it with water from the bathroom and arranges the flowers. He looks out of the window at the beach, focusing on something specific. He rolls up a mattress which is outside on the balcony and puts it away in the same cupboard. He leaves the cupboard door unlocked. He stands and admires the room.

WHITCHELL: Lovely.

He looks at his watch. He takes a scrap of paper from his pocket and dials a number on the phone.

(*On the phone.*) Good evening love… Eddie Whitchell. Now, first things first, this is a freephone number in't it?… now you don't know me, I've never rung before. I've thought about it, but I've not been inspired to make the effort until today. I live in Brid. Bridlington and one of your drivers has just come through town… No, no. I took a note of the number on the back and I thought I'd ring and give you my opinion, and it's an opinion worth having cos I used to drive a three ton fish truck mesen... Right love, have you gorra pen?... I'd say that your driver is driving courteously, observing the highway code, and driving with due regard and concern for the other road users and the pedestrians. So all in all very good, ten out of ten, and nothing to complain about at all... I'm a pedestrian. For instance at the roundabout down by the Spa where Bobby Davro's playing he stopped the lorry completely even though it's only a give way, cos he realised that the pedestrian crossing there is caught in a blind spot with the new toilets they've built with the European money they got, and we've had two people knocked down already this year and we don't want Bobby Davro to be the third do we?... You're entitled to your own opinion love. I was under the impression he's very popular with the ladies... You'd rather give birth to a chair, really, each to his own, her own. Me, I think that needless loss of life is best avoided at all times, whether it's a talented variety artist or, to use your phrase, an irritating little shit. Mind you if one of them graffiti vandals were to get knocked down then I'd be the first to celebrate. If I had my way I'd lock them up and throw away the door... Yes, I have finished, I think that's all I wanted to say, so er... it's a 'well done' to your driver fellah when you see him, 'very good', I was impressed... Tarra.

He puts the phone down.

(*He sighs.*) Shit, shower, shave. Bag up me smokes. No. Bag up me smokes, shit, shower, shave.

He sits and takes the old carrier bag and empties the contents on to the coffee table top. It is a fairly substantial pile of cigarette ends. He takes a set of scales from the cupboard and puts them on the coffee table. He sits and quickly and skilfully tears the filter from each tab and places the tobacco in the centre of a folded lottery ticket which sits on the scales.

Laughter off. A joyful scream. Followed by the fumbling of a key in the lock. IRENE and EDDIE stand on the threshold of the room. WHITCHELL does not react to their presence. IRENE is an attractive girl of about eighteen and is dressed in the fashions of 1955. She carries a cheap suitcase, and a bunch of flowers. There is confetti in her hair. EDDIE is also eighteen. He is of medium height, stocky, and muscular. He is dressed in a powder blue suit. His hair is done in a Brylcreemed DA style. His suitcase, an old cardboard one, is held together by a belt.

EDDIE: (*Surprised, pleased and impressed.*) Kaw!

IRENE: (*Surprised, pleased and moved.*) Bloody hell!

EDDIE: Kaw!!

IRENE: Oh it's smashin. Oh Eddie, it's bloody lovely.

EDDIE: (*Spots the champagne.*) Kaw!!!

He takes the bottle out of the bucket.

IRENE: Is that champagne Eddie?

EDDIE: (*Looking closely at the label, reading.*) Dom Perignon. Brut.

IRENE: Is it real champagne, or just fizzy wine?

EDDIE: How do I know? You're the doctor.

He hands the bottle over.

IRENE: It's real! Oh, Eddie how much did this cost me dad?

EDDIE: Aye, he's done us proud. How do you open 'em?

IRENE: Oh, I would know wunt I. Spent me whole life opening champagne bottles.

EDDIE: Sarcy.

He puts the bottle back in the ice bucket. He looks at the chandelier, then opens the French windows.

'kinnel.

He looks up and down the beach until he focuses on a point off – upstage right. He turns looking pleased with himself and closes the windows.

IRENE: It's like worr I dreamt of int it?

EDDIE: It's not good enough.

IRENE: You what?

EDDIE: (*Straight faced.*) It's not good enough for you Irene.

IRENE: Eddie! There's nowt wrong with it – it's lovely. It's perfect!

EDDIE: Nowhere's good enough for you.

IRENE: You'll talk yersen into heaven you will.

EDDIE: I am in heaven.

IRENE: God I love you Eddie Whitchell.

EDDIE: And I love you Mrs Whitchell.

They kiss. It is a sensuous kiss. He engineers her over to the bed and they fall on to it still kissing. She is underneath and he lies on top of her and he grinds his crotch into hers, and begins to undo her coat buttons. She pulls away from him. He lies back showing some frustration. He adjusts his tackle.

IRENE: D'yer think there's a bathroom?

EDDIE: (*Worried.*) Are you on?

IRENE: I'm not gonna go and get mesen wed at the wrong time of the month am I?

EDDIE: We can still do it even if you're on.

IRENE: Don't be disgusting.

(*Indicating the cupboard door.*) Is that a bathroom?

EDDIE leaps from the bed and tries to open the cupboard door. He turns the handle and pulls hard.

EDDIE: Locked.

He goes over to the bathroom door and opens it and peeks in.

Agh!

He goes in.

(*Off.*) Kaw! Eh, Irene come and have a look at this.

EDDIE flushes a loo needlessly, and turns on a tap or two. IRENE goes over, and into the bathroom.

IRENE: (*Off.*) Oh, this is smashing. What the bloody hell is that?

EDDIE: (*Off.*) French int it? For washing yer bits, you know, after.

IRENE: (*Off.*) After what?

EDDIE: (*Off.*) After the bloody cup final, what d'yer think?

IRENE: (*Off.*) I have dreams about bathrooms like this. It's like an 'ollywood one int it. Oh Eddie, I'm so happy.

EDDIE: (*Off.*) I'll get you a bathroom like this, bigger than this. We'll gerr our own house an'all. And a garden. Whatever you want. What do you want Irene?

IRENE: (*Off.*) A bit of privacy right now.

EDDIE leaves the bathroom kissing IRENE all the way to the door. She locks the door behind her. EDDIE hears this. He adjusts his tackle once again, and tries the door. It is locked.

EDDIE: Don't lock the door Irene. We're married aren't we?

IRENE: (*Off.*) I'm not having you watching.

EDDIE laughs. During the next he tests the temperature of the champagne and lies back on the bed. He gets off the bed and goes to listen at the bathroom door. He puts an ear up to the door, and finger in his other ear. He then goes back to the bed. He takes out a box of matches. He takes out four matches, sticks two in either side of the box, like shafts on a horse and cart. He puts a third match between the two shafts like a cross beam and lights the middle of it. He watches it burn down, and then jump. He laughs, and does it again. He continues this during the next.

WHITCHELL stands and puts the one ounce of tobacco in its paper wrap into the cupboard – for WHITCHELL the cupboard door is not locked. He takes the bag of useless tabs out into the hallway, but is only gone for a second or so before returning. He goes into the bathroom, which for him is unlocked, and turns on the taps to the bath. He comes out and strips down to his underpants. He has a faded tattoo of a panther's head on his left shoulder. Then he stands up very close to the wall down stage left and hums a low meditative hum. He continues this during the next.

Animated talk is heard coming from the corridor off. A key turns in the door. The door opens and TITS and IZZY stand in the doorway. TITS is a man of 43, overweight, dressed in a camel-hair coat and good business suit. IZZY is a 43-year-old woman, well dressed in expensive clothes, and with a rather elaborate hair-do. She carries a small quality leather suitcase, and he carries a matching, but larger, quality suitcase. He steps aside to let her into the room first.

TITS: Me own daughter! Me own bloody flesh and bloody blood gobbing, spitting, at the prime minister!

IZZY: Just let it lie will yer!

TITS: I'm sorry Izz, burr it's upset me. The prime minister! Not just any old prime minister either, the bloody finest prime minister this country's ever had. A woman an'all! A woman prime minister. On telly!

(*Stopping and looking a the room in awe.*) Bloody hell!

IZZY: It's just the same!

TITS: I told yer.

TITS puts his suitcase down, and looks at the phone. He lights a cigar, and surveys the room.

IZZY: They've not changed a thing!

TITS: I said, dint I? Yeah, it's the tits, int it, this room.

TITS goes over to feel the champagne. He organises two glasses. TITS sits by the phone.

IZZY: Same curtains aren't they? They've hardly faded. And the carpet's the same. Nothing's changed at all Eddie.

TITS: I bet this bed's tekken some hammer. Eh!? Ha, ha! Kaw! I wouldn't mind being a fly on the wall in this room. I bet they fight for that job.

TITS looks at his watch and picks up the phone to check if there is a dialling tone. There is and he puts it straight back down. IZZY has noticed this.

IZZY: Are you expecting a call?

TITS: Me? No. What a phone call? No. It's working though. Kaw! Our room eh? It's the duck's quack int it?

TITS starts to open the champagne.

IZZY: It's lovely.

TITS: D'yer know what I'd change if we buy this place? Go on guess.

IZZY: I stopped guessing twenty-five years ago.

TITS: The architrave. Architrave attracts muck like a cow's arse attracts bulls.

He runs a wetted finger along a run of picture rail.

Look at that. Filth.

During the next he pours a glass of champagne for IZZY and pours a glass of whisky from a quart bottle for himself.

IZZY: I don't think you, we, should buy this hotel.

TITS: Look, we gorra get out of fish ant we?

IZZY: Yeah.

TITS: I've had a look over the books. Not exactly the Yukon, but it's gorr its head above water.

He passes her a glass of champagne, and raises his own glass.

To us. To twenty five years of marriage, happiness, struggle, understanding, very poor decorating, ha! er… teamwork, loyalty, and love.

They clink glasses and drink. TITS slugs down his whisky and immediately goes off to the loo, leaves the door open, and pisses noisily and heartily.

The phone rings.

IZZY: There's your call. Who is it?

TITS: (*Still pissing.*) I'm not expecting owt.

IZZY: Do you want me to answer it?

TITS: (*Still pissing.*) I can't can I?

IZZY: (*On the phone.*) Hello?… Yes, he's here, hang on.

TITS comes in doing up his fly.

Can I speak to Tits?

TITS: (*On the phone.*) Now then horror bollocks – how's it going?… Oh fuck… No! Don't! Are yer mad? Give it half an hour. He's probably gorra bird in there or summat.

(*To IZZY.*) Gorra break in at Subway Street.

(*On the phone.*) Wait till he's off site. Ring back. We're eating here, in the hotel. Right, don't have a go!… Why not?

(*To IZZY.*) Jesus Christ! Whaddyerdo?

(*On the phone.*) Cos he'll kill yer cos yer pissed out yer box. Francis, have you ever noticed a pile of shit on top of me head?… Right, so what makes you think I'm a fucking idiot then… Just stay out of sight, and try not to breathe. He might smell you hiding. You an't got that dog of yours with yer have yer?… Good. Tarra.

He puts the phone down. Sits on the bed, looks at the phone chewing his nails. He feels the bottle of champagne.

IZZY: Francis Wiles?

TITS: Yeah, reckons Yebsley's on site nicking tools.

IZZY: Who's Yebsley?

TITS: Kid I laid off last year.

IZZY: Has Francis called the police?

TITS: If I had my way I'd lock him up and throw away the door.

IZZY: What kind of a name is Yebsley?

TITS: He did his apprenticeship with Yorkshire Electricity Board.

IZZY: Oh right. We're eating downstairs then? Not Giovanni's?

TITS: I've booked the table for eight o'clock. I thought we'd go to G's tomorrow.

IZZY: He's not open Sundays. You know he isn't.

TITS: I do don't I. Brain dead. Sorry love. Eh, it'll give us a chance to, you know, get the feel of the catering side of the operation.

IZZY: How is Francis nowadays?

TITS: Manic depression innit. He's up and down like a wanker's elbow. An't worked for two year now. Sleeps rough. One-off cash job this. Security.

TITS picks up the champagne and tops up her glass. TITS raises his glass for another toast.

Yer dad. Can't forget your dad. Not here. Bunny Wilson!

IZZY: Yeah. Dad!

They clink glasses and drink.

TITS: I miss the old bugger Izz. I know he dint like me, but he was straight, yeah, you knew where you stood with your dad. Out in the bloody yard usually. Ha!

IZZY: I know why you want to buy this place, Eddie. I can see right through you, like a window.

TITS: Ha! Aye, that's me – a slightly mucky window.

He drinks again. IZZY has sat on the bed and has begun to sniff, fighting back tears. TITS goes to the bathroom and comes back with some loo paper which he gives to her. TITS hands her the loo paper but knows that she cannot be consoled.

They've still got that bidet. I might have a go on there this time.

TITS moves away from her. During the next IZZY goes into the bathroom and closes the door. TITS looks at the phone, then at his watch, then lights a cigar, and unpacks.

EDDIE, now impatient, goes to the bathroom door, which for him is locked. He tries it unsuccessfully.

EDDIE: Irene! You alright?

IRENE: What's the matter with you Eddie?

EDDIE: I'm worried about yer.

IRENE: What you worried about?

EDDIE: Dunno.

EDDIE goes back to the bed, and flops down on it.

WHITCHELL stops the humming and goes into the bathroom (for him the door is unlocked) and turns the taps off. He gets into the bath and a long low sigh is heard.

There is the flush of a loo and IRENE comes out of the bathroom. She opens the windows and looks out. EDDIE watches her from the bed and then joins her at the window.

IRENE: Oh it's lovely here.

EDDIE: Can you see owt, on the beach?

He squeezes her breasts and bottom from behind.

IRENE: What? No. Gerroff! No, I can't.

EDDIE: (*Pointing.*) Over there.

IRENE: Oh! Eddie.

EDDIE: Can you see it?

IRENE: 'I love Mrs Whitchell.' Was that you?

EDDIE: While you were in the loos on the prom.

IRENE: Oh Eddie.

They kiss.

The tide'll wash it away.

EDDIE: I'm gonna write it out fresh every night we're here.

IRENE: Oh Eddie.

They kiss. He tries to move things along. She pulls away.

I can't believe this. The chandelier. A bathroom in the bedroom. Bit different from Strickie Ave eh?

EDDIE: I said, I'll gerr us an 'ouse with a bathroom, and a garden, and whatever you want Irene. I'll gerr it for you.

IRENE: I'd like a bathroom in the bedroom Eddie.

EDDIE: I'm not sure them plumbers in Hull are up to it, they've only just got the hang of hot water. I bet even Harold Needler ant gorra bog in the bedroom.

IRENE: I don't care what Harold Needler has.

EDDIE: You see you've got to have at least two doors between you, wherever you are, and a bog. Imagine you're in the living room, you can't just turn round, open one door, and there's the bog, you have to open one door, go in, whatever it is, little lobby thing, then open another door before you get to the bog. Building regulations they're called. I'll put it on the list. Chandelier, radiators, stainless steel sink, gravel drive. Bloody hell.

IRENE: Me dad's pushed the boat out for us ant he?

EDDIE: Aye, he has that.

She starts crying.

EDDIE: Eh, come on love.

IRENE: (*Crying.*) He ant got this sort of money.

EDDIE: Mebbe he had a good trip.

IRENE: (*Crying.*) He ant never had owt like this in his whole life. Nothing near. And the reception an'all.

EDDIE: You're his only daughter. Bride's father alles pays. I went to that Kathy Dixon's reception last year, and she's the youngest of seven sisters, int she. Poor do? Kaw! Terrible. Three blokes were killed fighting over a fish paste sandwich.

IRENE: (*Sobbing.*) Dad goes back tomorrow. Three days off he's had, and then back to sea for another three weeks.

EDDIE: (*Surreptitiously.*) He loves it.

IRENE: What?

(*Beat.*) He likes you Eddie. He told me.

EDDIE: Is that why he put me in hospital last year?

IRENE: You had your hand up me dress.

EDDIE: He never give me chance to explain.

IRENE: He liked your speech. I saw him laughing.

EDDIE: He's a deckie and deckies don't like us bobbers.

IRENE: That joke Francis told about the vicar and the nun.

EDDIE laughs.

EDDIE: How did the vicar get the nun pregnant?

IRENE: Shush! He should never have told that sort of joke at a wedding reception. Not with the vicar there. And them nuns from the Bethel. Where did he learn a joke like that?

EDDIE: He dint tell it that well.

IRENE: It was disgusting.

EDDIE laughs.

EDDIE: Your dad was laughing at that one. Him and his deckie mates. There was nearly a fight on Wednesday between us bobbers and the deckies. The mate of the Arctic Diamond accused a gang of bobbers of nicking fifty kit of haddock. He's a character, everyone calls him Stabba. D'yer know why? Go on, guess.

IRENE: Stabba? I dunno.

EDDIE: Cos he's got a thing he ses all the time. 'Stab-a-sausage!'

IRENE: How was I supposed to guess that? You want your head testing.

EDDIE: He's going 'Fuck me, stabbasausage, I had two thousand fucking kit off Bear Island, and as soon as I bastard dock in Hull, stabbasausage, fifty fucking kit goes bastard walkabout.' I've tekken the worst of the swearing out for you there. He gorr his way an'all.

IRENE: So they had nicked fifty kit then?

EDDIE: There's alles a lot of fish going missing.

IRENE: So the crew missed out on the money for that fifty kit?

EDDIE: Fifty was a bit much I have to admit, Mrs Whitchell.

They kiss and then break up. EDDIE lies back on the bed and stares at the ceiling. IRENE joins him but stares more at the chandelier.

TITS has finished unpacking. He has taken from his bag a small presentation box. He goes to the bathroom door and listens with his ear close up to the door and one finger in the other ear, the box in his hand.

IZZY: (*Off.*) Go away!

TITS sits back down.

EDDIE: (*Thoughtfully.*) I'd like me own catchphrase. Meks you a bit of a character.

He grapples with her clothes again and she stops him.

IRENE: It int dark yet.

EDDIE: Why's it gorra be dark?

IRENE: How I imagined it.

EDDIE: (*With sarcasm.*) I'll close the curtains then and turn the lights off.

They kiss. IRENE breaks it up, and stares at the chandelier.

IRENE: They're like tears.

EDDIE: What?

IRENE: Those bits of glass, like happy tears.

EDDIE: No such thing as happy tears.

IRENE: Do you know what glass is made from Eddie?

EDDIE: Load of sand all crushed up. I dunno.

IRENE: And where d'yer think sand comes from?

EDDIE: Off the beach, in the ground, quarries.

IRENE: Each grain of sand comes from a rock, and each rock at one time came from a mountain. Do you know what reduces a mountain?

EDDIE: Wind. Rain. Irresponsible ramblers.

IRENE: Tut! No. Time. The sand that made that tear there came from a rock which came from a mountain before any of those ages we did at school. Jurassic, Triassic, Devonian. That mountain is now our chandelier. Time. I will love you forever Eddie Whitchell.

EDDIE: Till death us do part.

IRENE: No. Forever. Infinity. Beyond death.

EDDIE: You're too clever for me.

IRENE: There's cats on my curtains.

EDDIE: There's dogs on my wall.

He kisses her and they slip into an extended kiss during which they overbalance and slip off the bed and end up on the floor upstage of the bed and out of sight. TITS gets up and taps the radiators. He then paces out the size of the room. IZZY comes out of the loo.

TITS: Izz. I got you summat. Just a little summat. You know, for the last twennie five years.

He passes the box over. She takes it.

You can open it now. I'd rather you opened it now, than in the restaurant.

IZZY: What is it Eddie?

TITS: It's nowt much, more – what do you call it? – symbolical. It won't explode. If it does I'll tek it back. Ha! Go on then, open up.

She opens the present. It is a simple silver wedding ring set with a single glorious diamond.

40

IZZY: Eddie.

TITS: It's silver innit, you know, for the twenty five, and er… that's a diamond.

IZZY: Oh God.

TITS: I'd like to think of it as a wedding ring. Cos, you know, I couldn't afford worr I wanted for you fost time round could I? Not to say that that band from Boysez was cheap, cos it want, but two pound ten was all I could afford when I was a bobber but things have changed ant they, and I'm not expecting you to replace the band with this one, except mebbe for functions you know, show it off a bit mebbe. I mean even the Queen dunt wash up with her fucking diamonds on does she. Ha! Occasions, mebbe, you know. D'yer like it?

IZZY: How much did it cost?

TITS: Arm and a leg.

IZZY: I can tell. I can't take it Eddie.

TITS: Like I say, I'm not trying to replace the band, that'll alles be the real one like, this is – what I say, symbolical. It's not the money, the money's nowt, the band is more important than this, course it is, alles will be, you know. I'm not suggesting we replace the old un.

IZZY: I can't take it Eddie.

He holds her. She is crying.

TITS: Come on. Come on. Whatsamatter? You deserve a bloody sight more than a little diamond.

IZZY: I don't deserve this. I don't deserve it.

(*Beat.*) Eddie, you know my Tuesdays and Thursdays?

TITS sits.

TITS: Oh no. Oh no don't. Oh God no. I know what you're gonna say. Don't say owt Izz. Don't talk. Don't say anything. Oh no, no, no.

Silence.

IZZY: I –

TITS: – I'm not listening! Don't talk!

Silence.

I feel funny. Summat's happening. Oh God. I'm shekkin. Oh God, oh God, oh God. No.

He goes to the window and opens it sucking in fresh air and undoing his tie.

Look, I'm shekkin.

IZZY: I'm sorry.

TITS: I'm shekkin! Look, I'm shekkin!

IZZY: You're not. You're not shaking.

TITS: I am. I'm shekking!

IZZY: You're trying to make yourself shake! Stop it Eddie please.

TITS: (*Shouting.*) I'm shekkin!

IZZY: Don't do this Eddie!

TITS: Look! I'm shekkin!

She slaps him hard across the face. He stops shaking.

Silence.

IZZY: Sorry.

TITS: Sorry. I'll be alright. Gimme a minute.

TITS takes a drink of scotch. EDDIE and IRENE pull out of a kiss, and sit up.

EDDIE: Twatinahat. Worrabout that one? Catchphrase. Problem is the first bit becomes your nickname. 'Twat'. I'll think of summat.

IRENE: When did you know that you loved me Eddie?

EDDIE: Doing the eleven plus test. I had a very funny thing happen to me. Don't tell no-one will you Irene?

IRENE: Cross me heart and hope to die.

EDDIE: This thing happens to people when they get hung, you know murderers. Miss Naylor said 'you have five minutes to go, please check through your answers.' And I'd only just got half way through. I felt myself getting hard, you know, a hard on, a really hard hard on.

IRENE: Did anyone see?

EDDIE: Dunno. I was scared, and you'd finished, and put your pencil down, and I knew then that you'd passed and that I'd failed, so we'd get split up, get sent to different schools, and I wouldn't see you every day. And then I shot it, you know, I fetched.

IRENE: You had an orgasm?

EDDIE: Yeah, like a dead man gets when he gets hung.

IRENE: Oh no.

EDDIE: I was only ten or eleven. There wan't any mess.

EDDIE gets up and goes to check the temperature of the champagne. IRENE pulls herself up and walks about the room redoing buttons which EDDIE has undone.

EDDIE: Irene? I was going to lose you, don't you see? Not see you every day.

IRENE: (*With her back to him.*) I think it's hanged, not hung.

EDDIE: You're disappointed it's not lovey dovey enough.

IRENE: No. It's a really romantic story. Just a bit disgusting.

He goes to her and holds her.

Sorry.

EDDIE: I've never had to mek anything up with you. It's the truth, cos it is, it's true. I couldn't smarm anything up any road could I? I'll never lie to you Irene. I promise you that.

IRENE: And I'll never lie to you Eddie. Never ever.

They kiss and make up, and go into a serious clinch.

TITS: There's someone at your night class.

IZZY: Yes.

Silence.

We're sleeping together.

Silence.

TITS: Why?

IZZY: I just am. It happened.

TITS: I don't gerrit.

IZZY: I couldn't stop myself.

TITS: But. You're married to me.

IZZY: I know.

TITS: Dunt that count for owt?

IZZY: I didn't want it to happen. I didn't make it happen.

TITS: What's his name?

IZZY: Martin Shanks.

TITS: Shanks.

(*Beat.*) Last Sunday afternoon? We had sex. We're having sex all the time. I don't understand.

Silence.

IZZY: I saw him this morning. We went to Infirmary. His mother's ill.

TITS: What's his fucking mother got to do with anything?!

IZZY: I'm sorry. It's not anyone's fault this. It's something that just happened.

TITS: Well it int my fault!

(*Beat.*) Pick yer days don't yer. Why not yesterday? Or tomorrow?

IZZY: Today, now, is the first time it's really felt wrong.

TITS: So, you don't love me no more?

IZZY: I didn't say that. I don't know.

TITS: Well I love you, I know I do, I always have, and I always will. I don't care what you do or what you've done.

IZZY: Love. The word has no mystery for you, does it?

TITS: (*Angry.*) No it dunt. You love someone, you can feel it, like a lump, summat you carry around with yer. Bloody hell, it's either there or it int, like a hat. You read too much bloody poetry that's your trouble. I've never loved no-one else. I don't think I'm capable.

IZZY: I'm not as uncomplicated as you Eddie. I'm complicated.

TITS: I'm gonna go out. I've got summat to do, that I ant got round to doing yet. Summat to do with our silver wedding.

He goes out.

45

Enter WHITCHELL from the bathroom. He has a towel wrapped around his waist. He has a pint glass about half full of a yellow liquid. He sits on the bed and dresses in a strange cocktail of clothes – Chinese shoes, white linen Gandhi-style trousers, and a Japanese dressing gown.

IRENE fights off EDDIE who is trying to move things forward. EDDIE turns away, disgruntled, and turns his attention to the champagne, which for him is a full unopened bottle.

EDDIE: Bit cawlder.

IRENE: Sorry Eddie. I'll be alright. I'm just a bit scared.

EDDIE: Yeah, yeah. Bloody hell, what do you do?

EDDIE puts the bottle on the floor and tries to pull the cork out, holding the bottle secure between his legs. He strains, and fails.

Fuck.

IRENE: Don't swear. We're being posh.

EDDIE now twists the cork, and finds that it gives.

EDDIE: Eh, up. Here we go. Gerr a glass.

The cork pops. IRENE is excited and thrilled. EDDIE pours champagne unskilfully for IRENE and himself. It overflows the glasses.

Agh! Bloody hell. Fizzy int it?

IRENE: It's not beer.

EDDIE: Ugh.

IRENE: Oh wow! This is perfect Eddie.

EDDIE: Yeah, it's the duck's quack.

He burps.

Gassy int it?

He puts the bottle back in the bucket. They kiss. EDDIE makes a move on the buttons. Again IRENE stops him.

EDDIE: It is our wedding night you know.

IRENE: I want it to get a bit darker. I always imagined it would be night time. I'll be alright.

EDDIE: Not sure I will.

IRENE: How d'yer mean?

EDDIE: Gerrin a bit of love nut. System starts backing up after a bit dunt it.

He stands adjusts his tackle, and touches his toes a couple of times.

IRENE: Have you got any johnnies?

EDDIE: Jesus Christ on a raft! Johnnies? You do want kids don't yer?

IRENE: Not in nine months' time I don't no!

EDDIE: You got sacked from the chocolates cos Needler found out you're gonna get wed and that means you're gonna be carrying a bain soon enough. So let's hear no more about that.

IRENE: You ant gorr any johnnies then?

EDDIE: No.

He lights a cigarette, thinking.

(*Beat.*) Jesus Christ on a raft. Whaddyerthink of that one Irene? Me uncle Ted ses that sometimes. 'Jesus Christ on a raft! Did that horse win?' 'Jesus Christ on a raft – she's been and gone and dyed her hair'.

IRENE: They'd end up calling you Jesus.

EDDIE: Aye. I'll go and get some johnnies.

He kisses her passionately again, then bends down and touches his toes twice, then leaves quickly. IRENE unpacks. She takes a penguin novel, from her bag, and puts it on the bedside table. She looks out of the window at the writing in the sand, then goes to the bed and curls up with the book, facing downstage.

WHITCHELL has decided on a Chinese-style embroidered hat and leather Arabic slippers with pointy toes, no socks. There is a knock at the door. WHITCHELL looks at his watch, then opens the door. Baroness MARFLEET stands in the doorway. She is an impressive-looking woman of about 65, dressed in a quality two-piece suit, not a business suit but we can imagine that she would be comfortable in a barristers' chambers, or the House of Lords. She carries a black leather briefcase, and a large key on a lump of wood.

MARFLEET: Hello Eddie.

WHITCHELL: Hello Irene. Are you coming in?

MARFLEET: I've come from Belgium.

WHITCHELL: You'd better come in then.

She bends towards him and kisses him lightly on the lips.

What d'yer call that?

MARFLEET: A kiss.

WHITCHELL: I've had more fun syphoning petrol.

MARFLEET: It's all you're getting.

WHITCHELL: You always give in! Here. The stustistics are on my side. In quarter of an hour, I guarantee, we'll be rolling about on that bed.

MARFLEET: When did you last have sex?

WHITCHELL: Last year. I wanted to celebrate the Queen's Jubilee.

MARFLEET: Who was that with then?

WHITCHELL: Layla. Nice little lass at the Sauna and Massage.

MARFLEET: A prostitute?

WHITCHELL: No, no. She's the receptionist, but she helps out if they get busy.

MARFLEET: Lovely shoes.

WHITCHELL: Thank you.

MARFLEET: My mother always used to say you can judge a man by his shoes.

WHITCHELL: Rubbish.

MARFLEET: She was right about Gary Glitter.

MARFLEET hands over the key.

I locked it after me.

WHITCHELL: Good. Crime! Kaw! Terrible. Do you remember down Strickie Ave you could leave your back door open. Nothing ever got stolen.

MARFLEET: We had bugger all worth nicking.

They laugh together.

WHITCHELL: Tin bath. You're swearing nowadays then?

MARFLEET: You've changed.

WHITCHELL: I've changed?! Look who's calling the kettle black.

MARFLEET: Why didn't you write? Not even a card.

WHITCHELL: You don't write to your own wife. That's inviting disaster.

MARFLEET: I sent cards. Your birthday, every birthday.

WHITCHELL: Oh aye, women remember all the nice anniversaries don't they. What you never get is a card to celebrate the day you stopped shagging.

MARFLEET: Maybe you haven't changed.

WHITCHELL: Take your coat off.

She does. He takes it.

Champagne? It's what you drink here. I've got me own stuff.

WHITCHELL drinks, and opens the champagne, which is a new bottle with cork.

MARFLEET: There were quite a few firemen sitting out there.

WHITCHELL: That one with the tash has died. He was a Lithuanian. 'A man without a moustache, is like meat without mustard'. Old Lithuanian saying. Symbol of virility, masculinity, and success you see. Big tash, big man. Small tash, small man. No tash, nobody. They've discovered that hospital patients in Lithuania are much more relaxed in the operating theatre if their surgeon has a moustache, so they issue false moustaches to those surgeons who don't have one of their own. They buried him last week, and on Tuesday there's a memorial service, for the moustache.

MARFLEET: You're terrible you.

WHITCHELL: (*Raising his pint pot.*) Cheers! Bunny Wilson!

MARFLEET: Dad!

They drink, WHITCHELL from his pint glass.

WHITCHELL: You're lovely… bloody hell. Grand. Immaculate. Like a ship.

MARFLEET: I want –

WHITCHELL: – I know what you want! I've been expecting it. The answer's 'no'. An emphatic 'no' I think they call it.

MARFLEET: Oh Eddie, don't –.

WHITCHELL: – what am I supposed to call you? Nowadays.

MARFLEET: Irene. Or Izzy.

WHITCHELL: I read the papers you know. In the library.

MARFLEET: Well why do you ask then?

WHITCHELL: Baroness Marfleet. Kaw! What does that mek me?

MARFLEET: Eddie Whitchell.

They both laugh.

WHITCHELL: You got there then. Using yer brain. What did they give yer the title for? Sorting the Micks out?

MARFLEET: I guess so.

WHITCHELL: Bloody brilliant thing you did there. How did yer pull that off?

MARFLEET: I was lucky.

WHITCHELL: There's a lot of them that has had a go afore you and failed. Clever people an'all, couldn't even get the bastards to sit in the same fucking room. They tell me people are going back to live in Belfast, you know, them what had left. What are you working on now?

MARFLEET: Asylum policy. The integration of Refugee and Asylum policy across the –

WHITCHELL: Would you like a Cherry Bakewell? I picked some up this morning.

He winks.

MARFLEET: I hope you paid for them.

WHITCHELL: I nick stuff cos at my age you've got to find excitement and a hint of danger wherever you can. I can't have me ears syringed every day.

MARFLEET: You must tell me if you're short.

WHITCHELL: I'm down to bones of me bum. Asylum seekers eh? It wouldn't be so bad if every now and then you saw one of them with a brush in his hand. Muslims, they're alright if you need a pint of milk on a Christmas Day.

MARFLEET: Don't get me started Eddie!

WHITCHELL: We got one runs a shop on the corner. His daughter works in there, he won't let her go to school, she must be onny fourteen. I asked her if she had an artificial Christmas tree. She didn't know what the fuck I was talking about.

MARFLEET: Eddie!

WHITCHELL: Don't you fucking Eddie me! You're the one what wants a divorce. I've gorr all the cards.

MARFLEET: This is a game is it?

WHITCHELL: It's true in't it? What other reason would you want to see me for? After twennie odd year.

MARFLEET: I would have seen you before, I tried, many times.

WHITCHELL: But you wouldn't come here!

MARFLEET: No, can you blame me? Not to this room, no.

WHITCHELL: I live here!

MARFLEET: Do you sleep in the bed?

WHITCHELL: I don't go to bed. You die in bed. I sleep on the balcony. I'm an ascetic. Apparently. I eat hummus. Chick peas. Pythagoras said you can purify your soul if you enough beans. I keep the windows open.

MARFLEET: You always did like the windows open.

WHITCHELL: Drink. Nowt but the yellow stuff.

MARFLEET: What do you do all day?

WHITCHELL: Today, I cut the grass. Did a Wembley, all different patterns. The park keeper weren't too chuffed. They have a photo of me in their shed. I'm not saying I'm banned but they won't let me in the park if I've got the mower with me. I used to think they enjoyed the chase, but obviously not. It's only a hovver mower, it's nowt clever, it's not one of them you sit on, well you can sit on it, but if you did it wouldn't work. I'm learning mesen to levitate at the moment. You stand up very close to the wall, pick out a nick and concentrate very hard until you and the wall become one, and then you just rise up. I just had a go actually.

MARFLEET: Did it work?

WHITCHELL: No, but I felt a bit lighter.

MARFLEET: Are you well Eddie?

WHITCHELL: I'm seeing a bloke, a psychiatrist. Doctor something or other. I call him Doctor Doctor, which he says is very childish of me. I don't trust him. He's the sort of bloke who'd piss on yer chips. What's your intended's name?

MARFLEET: Mark Woolf.

WHITCHELL: Is he a big fellah?

MARFLEET: He's a pacifist.

WHITCHELL: I should win that one then. Don't look at me like that, I never laid a finger on Armitage.

MARFLEET: Yes, people often question the effectiveness of court orders but it certainly worked in that case.

WHITCHELL: I'll not divorce you.

MARFLEET: I don't need your permission. We've been separated for twenty-three years. But –

WHITCHELL: – I know, it'd be easier. I'll not give you a divorce, but I won't stand in your way either. I'll kill mesen.

MARFLEET looks at him. He looks serious, and committed to this course of action. She cannot find anything to say, and worried turns away and goes onto the balcony.

TITS enters. He has sand on his shoes.

IZZY: Sand.

TITS: I know, I know.

He takes his shoes off and goes to the balcony where he bangs them on the balcony rail, and whilst doing that has a look at his handywork.

That fireman's still there. That big long streak of shite with the tash. The foreign looking fellah. Got three pips on his shoulder now. One for every cat he's rescued. Who's he think he is? Why dunt he go indoors? What's he want – a bloody medal. Tut!

Silence.

Have a look at this one. It's a good un.

Silence.

Should last a while an'all. Tide's just turned. Med a rod
for me own back there dint I? What a honeymoon I had.
Every day, twice a bloody day out there scratching 'I
love Mrs Whitchell' in the sand. Ha! That shrimper used
to take the piss, ha! 'You're laughing now' he used to say.
'You just bloody wait'. Miserable old git. He was right
though wan't he? I'm gerrin summat wrong aren't I.
What's the score? Love 2 Eddie Whitchell nil.

IZZY: I aren't gonna talk about Harriet.

TITS: Lost you both ant I? Why does she hate me Izzy?

IZZY: I said. I aren't gonna talk about Harriet.

TITS: She's got no idea. Thinks Strickie Ave to Kirkella is a
fucking bus ride. Took us what, best part of fifteen years.
That's the longest, hardest, sloggiest bus ride there ever
was.

IZZY: Sloggiest?

TITS: Int that a word?

IZZY: No. Any road, I said, I aren't gonna talk about
Harriet.

TITS: I don't want 'grateful'. I just want to know, that she
knows, why for people like us, that's why we gorr out of
bed every morning.

IZZY: Just let her go Eddie.

TITS: I used to watch her in her cot. Scared she was dead.
Wanted to see the blanket twitch, you know, owt. It's that
shit they're filled her head with at school!

IZZY: (*Pedantically. She's corrected him on this many times.*)
University.

TITS: Now you hate me an'all.

IZZY: You hate things about me. Reading.

TITS: I don't hate it. We can't afford for both of us to be pig ignorant or we'd never get invited to them Kirkella dinner parties.

IZZY: We never do get invited to Kirkella dinner parties.

TITS: You're not reading enough then. Ha, ha! Got you there.

IZZY: I've only slept with Martin three times. I don't love him, and I don't hate you.

TITS: Kaw! We're having a funny day aren't we?

IZZY: How could I hate you, you idiot? You've been the whole of my life.

TITS: I can still see yer, you know.

IZZY: Don't! Eddie. Please!

TITS: Little lass, on a bogie, tidemark round her neck, mucky sannies. Her brothers teasing her, me and her going round the back off Salvesons, tekking our things off in a ditch. I have a look at her little fanny, and she looks at my willy. And I've gorra box of matches, and we light 'em all and try and set fire to the grass. And she's not much interested in me willy. She wants to look at me leg. Which one was it? Me right leg. She meks me tek me brace off. Med me try and walk without it. I had a bloody good go. Me dad braed hell out of me for tekking it off. Best thing that ever happened to me. Polio. It was my education.

IZZY: Don't use that word!

TITS: All that swimming, morning, noon, and night. It taught me everything I ever needed to know. The pain. Gerrin over it.

Silence.

Izz?

Silence.

TITS: Oh come on. Don't play that one.

Silence.

D'yer wanna eat? We still have to eat?

Silence.

I'll cancel the table then. Izz?

Silence.

Izzy?! Fuck.

MARFLEET enters from the balcony.

MARFLEET: Did you do that one yourself?

WHITCHELL: Aye. Went out about an hour back. Tide's turned but it's got another couple of hours to go. This light's good tonight. You can almost touch it. Like, silk. Beautiful.

MARFLEET: You won't kill yourself Eddie.

WHITCHELL: I will.

MARFLEET: No you won't.

WHITCHELL: Yes I will.

MARFLEET: No you won't.

WHITCHELL: Yes, I will. Creatively. Spectacularly. I'll find a way of doing it off the world wide web.

MARFLEET: Have you got the internet?

WHITCHELL: No. I'll go and get it tomorrow.

MARFLEET: I won't let you kill yourself. I won't marry if that's what it means.

WHITCHELL: But I want you to marry! I want it for you... I want what you want for yersen. I always have. That's... that's... I mean... that's always been it, an't it?

MARFLEET: Oh God. You mean it don't you?

She sits.

WHITCHELL: I didn't know whether it were over or not, that's all. You know, us.

MARFLEET: I know you love me, you –

WHITCHELL: I'm not gonna kill mesen to prove I love you.

MARFLEET: I still love you, you might not believe it but I do, but –

WHITCHELL: I don't even want you to love me. I'd drag you down.

MARFLEET: (*As a warning.*) Self-pity Eddie!

WHITCHELL: The truth! Brutal, bloody honest, bastard truth.

MARFLEET: Oh God I hate Yorkshiremen!

WHITCHELL: You're one yersen!

They laugh.

A woman one.

MARFLEET: Thank you.

WHITCHELL: How's Harriet? I lost her an'all didn't I.

MARFLEET: Self pity and Eddie Whitchell – that's your true marriage.

WHITCHELL: It's true int it? Cut her hair off. Changed her name. Harry – for a lass. Bonny lass an'all. How old is she now?

MARFLEET: Forty-three.

WHITCHELL: What does a forty-three-year-old lesbian with two sociology degrees do in this modern world.

MARFLEET: She runs a dry ski slope in Kettering.

They laugh and fall onto the bed.

TITS: Izz! I'm not gonna not talk you know! Not on me bloody wedding anniversary. Not talking. I'm not gonna do that. I'll talk to mesen if I have to. I'm gonna have a bloody good time I am. You godda eat something. Whaddyer want?

(*Beat.*) Tut!

Enter EDDIE with two large boxes of condoms. IRENE puts her book down, noting the page carefully. She turns to kiss him and he climbs on the bed and kisses her furiously.

EDDIE: I got some. Couple of dozen.

IRENE: What? Twennie four.

EDDIE: Yeah. Should be enough for tonight eh?

IRENE: I would hope so. Eh, have you been using johnnies with Helen Bradshaw?

EDDIE: She's just a slag.

IRENE: She's been 'just' a slag for three years.

EDDIE: She was just for sex.

IRENE: I bet you didn't tell her that?

EDDIE: As a matter of fact I did. I said as soon as Irene Wilson ses 'yes' I'm chucking you like a shitty stick.

IRENE: Did it hurt her – you know fost time you did it?

EDDIE: She want a virgin any road.

IRENE: No, course. What's the most you ever did it with her? In one go I mean?

EDDIE: I've never stayed a night with her. We used to go in that old bus –

IRENE: I know where you did it.

EDDIE: That's why this is so special. I mean this is the sort of bed what was med for sex. Look at it. Kaw! And I can sleep with you all night, together, and tomorrow an'all. Don't have to spend all night in the fish room of some stinking tub, scraping shit off the pounds boards. Fucking bollocking cawld.

IRENE: Don't swear Eddie!

EDDIE: It is cawld down there Irene.

IRENE: Cawld for me dad on deck an'all in the Arctic.

EDDIE: He loves it. Ha! You wouldn't catch me going deckie. Do you know who they're scared of? Go on, have a guess?

IRENE: I dunno.

EDDIE: I've seen a trawler come in with three thousand kit of best Iceland cod, and all the big dicks are there – trawler owner, skipper, mate, clapping each other on the back and then the little fish merchant comes along in his cap, with a little fag going, tells 'em there's over much fish on dock so's the whole trip'll go for fish meal. Aye, no-one's bigger than the market, and the market's always feast or famine.

TITS exits, taking his jacket with him.

MARFLEET: Helen Bradshaw.

WHITCHELL: What about her?

MARFLEET: She's dead.

WHITCHELL sits up.

WHITCHELL: Bloody hell.

MARFLEET: She got a big, miniature, cherry tomato stuck in her throat.

WHITCHELL: A big, miniature, cherry, tomato?

MARFLEET: Yes. It was bigger than it should've been.

WHITCHELL: Fucked her good and proper then. That's all she ever wanted.

They laugh.

EDDIE: Do you know what makes me different Irene? Guess.

IRENE: I'm sick of bloody guessing!

EDDIE: I know what I want. Most people don't know what they want. They say 'I wunt mind winning the pools', but they don't even do the bloody pools. They're happy living like animals. That's why I ant gorr any time for deckies, and I don't mean yer dad. They crawl out of Rayners go straight down dock, next minute they wake up off Iceland, they're gerrin fed and watered, told what to do, what to think, and then they come home after three weeks, get pissed up, get their lass up the duff, and then escape back to sea again.

IRENE: And mebbe not come back.

EDDIE: 'Course! In my book, the first thing you gorra do to improve yersen is gerr a job where you aren't gonna get killed. What is it yer dad ses – 'you're not buying fish, you're buying men's lives!'

IRENE: That was Sir Walter Scott.

EDDIE: No, I'm sure it was your dad.

(*Beat.*) I don't like firemen either.

IRENE: What you got against firemen?

EDDIE: Dunno. What is it when summat can't be explained?

IRENE: Irrational.

EDDIE: Did you see that one down on the promenade? The one with the tash. Thinks he's God's bloody gift. Standing there, doing nowt, in his wellies. I just don't like the whole idea of them.

IRENE: That doesn't make any sense.

EDDIE: It's irrational.

EDDIE kisses her, and they go into a gentle clinch.

MARFLEET: I knew if I came here something terrible would happen.

WHITCHELL: You can't blame the room. It's a fucking room. Four walls.

MARFLEET: You know what this room is.

WHITCHELL: You read to much, always did. Stories, stories, stories. Med up rubbish. You've med this room into a problem which it isn't.

MARFLEET: You've done exactly the same, in your own way, but you don't even know you've done it.

WHITCHELL: Oh aye, I'm the bloody mad one.

MARFLEET: It's not right Eddie. Taking your own life. People hang on to life. That lad last year in America, the mountaineer. He sawed his own arm off with a penknife.

WHITCHELL: Aye?

MARFLEET: Didn't you see it on the news?

WHITCHELL: I'm gonna get a new telly. Forty-six inch flat screen, plasma. Three thousand five hundred and ninety nine pounds. Comet.

MARFLEET: One of his arms was pinned by a boulder, in a rock fall. He tied a tourniquet around his arm and then, with a penknife, he sawed his arm off just below the elbow. He seemed driven by instinct to do the right thing. He even knew the names of all the bones.

WHITCHELL: Maybe he'd done it before.

MARFLEET laughs.

The phone rings. IZZY thinks for a moment and then picks it up.

IZZY: (*On the phone.*) Hello… yes, hello Francis, it's Izzy… No, he's just gone to get something to eat… yes, I'll tell him… Yebsley has gone. O.K. Have the police been?… the police, did you ring them?… right… right… Alright, I'll tell him Francis… Nice to talk to you… tarra.

She puts the phone down.

IRENE sits up.

IRENE: Eddie Whitchell – a fish merchant. Ha! You will be one then. If you've ever clapped eyes on owt you've gorr it in the end.

EDDIE: You.

They kiss. EDDIE now tries to get really passionate. IRENE fights him off.

IRENE: You're only a bobber though Eddie, and a fish room man at that, you're not even on dock. Who's ever heard of a bobber becoming a fish merchant?

EDDIE: I've bin supplying this chippie up in Driffield. Couple of chippies as it happens.

IRENE: You bin nicking fish?!

EDDIE: Half a kit a week. That's all he needs.

IRENE: Half a kit? That's five stone of fish. How d'yer gerr it up to Driffield? Not on yer bike that's for sure.

EDDIE: Francis has been lending me the carpet shop van.

IRENE: Eddie, it's wrong. It's not right.

EDDIE: Everyone's nicking off dock.

IRENE: Me dad int. In fact you're nicking from me dad, cos that half a kit is half a kit that dunt show in his money.

EDDIE gets off the bed in a mood and goes over to the window.

Who drives the van? You can't drive. I don't like the sound of this.

EDDIE: Driving's easy enough. I get there and back before it gets dark.

EDDIE is looking out of the window. He is now angry.

D'yer wanna live in Strickie Ave all your life? D'yer wanna car?!

IRENE: I can't drive. You can't drive.

EDDIE: I'm not gonna be a fucking bobber all me life! I'm gonna mek summat of meself – for you – if nowt else.

EDDIE goes into the bathroom and locks the door behind him. IRENE goes to the door and tries it but it is locked.

Enter TITS with a pizza and some After Eight mints.

TITS: Some pizza there.

Silence.

Oh fuck. Come on Izz. After eight mints an'all. Tut! I cancelled dinner. They had the table all decked out. Flowers. Huh. I said you weren't feeling well. It's about half full – the restaurant. Never thought that as well as your guests there's your walk-in customer an'all. Kaw! I got a bit to learn about hotelling. They gorra new pizza oven. Tekkin off int it? The new fish and chips. That's how Mario Lanza got fat. He used to piss in a bucket you know, on the set. Mario Lanza. Oh come on love!

(*Beat.*) If we buy this place, we get more than one business. You get your rooms business, your restaurant, and there's your conference facilities.

IRENE goes to listen at the bathroom door.

IRENE: Eddie! Open the door! Eddie! Whatsamatter? I'm sorry.

She then goes over to the bed and picks up her book but unable to concentrate puts it back down again.

MARFLEET: Kathy Dixon?

WHITCHELL: Dead?

MARFLEET: Hit and run driver, on the zebra outside Boyzes She was coming home from bingo. She'd won half a pound of liver.

WHITCHELL: They tell me there's a stern trawler fishing out of Hull.

MARFLEET: Not really. They catch their quota in a month, and then go to South Africa. There's no cod left Eddie.

WHITCHELL: We had it all eh?

MARFLEET: Yes.

The bathroom door opens and EDDIE enters the room. He enters slowly, guiltily. He sits on the downstage side of the bed. He flashes IRENE a false smile.

IRENE: You alright?

EDDIE: Me? Yeah.

IRENE: I'm sorry Eddie. Are you alright?

EDDIE: Yeah.

IRENE: Kiss me Eddie.

He kisses her dutifully, without enthusiasm.

What've you been doing in there?

EDDIE: I feel a lot better.

IRENE: What? The pain's gone?

EDDIE: Oh yes.

IRENE: Good. It's dark now.

EDDIE: Is it?

She kisses him. He's not very enthusiastic, but responds.

IRENE: Yes.

EDDIE: (*Deflated.*) Smashin.

IRENE: Shall we, now? Shall we do it?

EDDIE: Do what?

IRENE: I feel right. I'm ready now. I think.

EDDIE: Give me five minutes.

IRENE: What? Don't you want to do it?

EDDIE: Of course I bloody do. I'm just not ready yet. Let me have a drink, and a fag. I'll be with you in a tick.

IRENE: What?

EDDIE pours himself a drink of champagne and lights a cigarette, and collapses back on the bed, staring up at the chandelier. MARFLEET lies on the bed and stares up at the chandelier.

MARFLEET: Mountains.

WHITCHELL: Eh? Oh aye.

TITS: Three businesses. And of course we get our room, your dad's room thrown in. And some quality clobber, furniture and that, all over the place. You know, like your chandelier.

EDDIE: Glass eh?

TITS: Godda be worth a few bob eh?

WHITCHELL: I've had it valued.

TITS: This chandelier of yours.

WHITCHELL: Auctioneer. Well, he used to be an auctioneer.

TITS: Can't be plaggy. There's hardly owt that's plaggy in here.

IRENE: What do you think glass is Eddie? Solid, liquid or gas?

EDDIE: Yer mad. How can it be gas? Or liquid.

TITS: If it were a fucking fish I could tell yer worr it was worth. To the penny.

IRENE: It's not a solid.

TITS: Size. Weight. Has it gone off?

IRENE: It's not liquid either. Glass is somewhere in-between.

EDDIE: Bollocks.

TITS: Fifty quid at least. Big bastard int it? Mebbe sixty quid then. Foreign int it. Dutch mebbe. They like their lampshades, don't they, the Dutch? Tulips, lemon sole, and fancy arsed lampshades. Yes, definitely Dutch.

WHITCHELL: It's French. A copy of a Remi Picq design. Late eighteenth century, but pre-revolution.

TITS: If you heat glass up it liquefies. Turns back to nowt.

WHITCHELL: It's lead crystal.

MARFLEET: I always thought it was.

IRENE: It's just so beautiful.

TITS: You'll never believe this, but glass is neither solid nor liquid.

IZZY: I told you that!

TITS: Gotcha! You're talking!

IZZY: I was never not talking. I just had nothing to say. But I have now. Francis called. Yebsley has gone. Francis says he's 'getting on with it now'.

TITS: Tut!

IZZY: He hasn't called the police though.

TITS: Did he not? That's what I mean. Shit for brains.

IZZY: He sounded very, very, very tense.

TITS: Course he's tense. He's picked a bad night, the same night Yebsley's chosen to do his Christmas shopping. When did he ring?

IZZY: Why don't you call the police?

TITS: Yebsley's nowt. I'll get square with him.

IZZY: Answer me! Why don't you call the police?

TITS: Cos it's my silver wedding, and I'm having a fucking smashin time!

IRENE sits up.

EDDIE: Are you hungry?

IRENE: (*Sulking now.*) No, I aren't.

EDDIE: I'm a bit peckish. Do you want some chips? I'll go out and get some chips. There's a chippie not ten yards away. Chips and scratchings yeah? Or do you wanna nice bit of haddock?

IRENE: I'm not hungry Eddie.

EDDIE: A pattie then?

IRENE: Are yer deaf?

EDDIE: Won't be long. I'll get some whisky an'all. That champagne's given me the farts.

He leaves. She is deflated. MARFLEET sits on the downstage side of the bed next to WHITCHELL.

MARFLEET: Do you want to make love?

WHITCHELL: I can still do it.

MARFLEET: So can I.

WHITCHELL: You're beautiful. But you're a Baroness. It'd be like fucking the Queen.

MARFLEET: She does it as well.

WHITCHELL: Does she? Who with? Him?

MARFLEET: Yeah.

WHITCHELL: Bloody hell!

MARFLEET: Do you want to?

WHITCHELL: Let me think of all the implications. (*Quickly.*) Yes.

MARFLEET: Good.

WHITCHELL: Are you trying to save me life?

MARFLEET: Yes.

WHITCHELL: It won't work. It'll mek things worse.

MARFLEET: Alright. We won't do it then.

WHITCHELL: It might work.

They laugh. MARFLEET stands and takes her jacket off, and hangs it up in the wardrobe. She walks back to the bed. But stops and takes her dress off revealing a modest full length slip. He stands and lets her pull the covers back and get in. During the next he strips off down to his underpants.

IZZY: You're up to summat.

TITS: You're the one what's up to summat.

IZZY: Why is Francis doing security? You've got a contract with Securicor.

TITS: That's finished.

IZZY: Why?

TITS: Cos I ant paid 'em.

IZZY: Why haven't you paid them?

TITS: Cos I ant gorr any fucking money! I'm down to the bones of me bum.

MARFLEET: You've got a good body Eddie. You had a beautiful body when you were young.

WHITCHELL looks at his body in the mirror.

WHITCHELL: I'm almost back to it now. What's your blood pressure?

MARFLEET: Hundred and sixty over ninety.

WHITCHELL: (*Whistles.*) Bit high. Hundred and fifty over eighty five. Swimming, diet. I drink me own urine too. Twice a day. You should try it. Not mine. Your own.

MARFLEET: What's it like?

WHITCHELL: Terrible. Tastes like piss.

MARFLEET: There's cats on my curtains.

WHITCHELL: There's dogs on my wall.

WHITCHELL and MARFLEET kiss and go into a passionate embrace underneath the covers. During the next they make love.

TITS: We're skint. There's no cod left Izz. Hull's finished.

IZZY: So you've decided to buy a hotel.

TITS: I've got some assets.

IZZY: You're selling the cold store?

TITS: No-one in their right mind would buy a cold store in Hull at the moment. No. I'm having it burnt down. Francis. Insurance.

IZZY: You stupid bastard Eddie. You'll go to prison.

TITS: No I won't. Francis will. That's the deal. He admits to doing it. I give him two grand for every month he does inside.

IZZY: What makes you think you can buy a man's life?!

TITS: I come from Hull! That's all fishing is and ever fucking was! Men's lives!

IZZY: They'll not fail to see you behind this.

TITS: Nowt to do with me. I'm here aren't I? I'm in Brid.

IZZY: You bastard. This. Our anniversary, and it's just an alibi for you!

She starts hitting him across the face. Big slaps which he just takes and makes absolutely no attempt to protect his face, or stop her.

TITS: We were coming here anyway!

IZZY: The ring!

TITS: No. No. No. You're wrong.

IZZY: You bastard! You bastard Eddie!

TITS: No!

IZZY: You've used me!

TITS: No!

IZZY: Bastard.

She hits him one last time and collapses on the bed crying.

Where's that little boy gone? The boy with the stick leg. I so loved him. Why couldn't you have learned to live with it? I wunt have thought any the less of you. But no you have to go and beat it, learn to bloody swim, and build the muscles, and get ruthless, and pig headed, and pig ignorant, and hard, and all the other words that describe the man I'm left with.

TITS: I did it for you.

IZZY: Don't say that!

TITS: Everything I've ever done I've done for you.

IZZY: That's something you've heard in a song.

TITS: No! I fucking loved having a brace. I only got rid of it to prove to you that I had summat. I wan't brainy enough for you was I? So I swam. I swam, and swam, and swam, and swam, and swam, and swam, and fucking swam! I know the ceiling of them baths down Albert Ave better than I know me own face. And this, buying this hotel is for you. If we don't gerrit, someone else will, and what will they do with it? Who knows? They might gut it. Tear out this room, your dad's room, this bed, the chandelier.

IZZY: This is not my dad's room! Don't call it that! How many times have I told you! Jesus Christ!

IZZY goes to the loo and locks the door behind her.

TITS: Yeah, yeah. Go on. Off you go.

WHITCHELL climaxes with a groan, almost painful. MARFLEET is silent.

Silence.

WHITCHELL: (*Beat.*) Frances Wiles.

MARFLEET: Dead?

WHITCHELL: Yeah. Struck by lightning.

MARFLEET: In Canada?

WHITCHELL: Yes. I don't think he'd made any friends out there. He kept a few chickens but lived off the social really. But then a couple of year back this drugs research company paid him to wear this strip of magnesium on the top of his head for a year. Cos he was bald remember, they wanted to see if over the course of time the skin would take in this magnesium, you know like suck it in, and regenerate the pores of the scalp, cos the skin breathes of course. And they tell me it was a big patch like a six inch ruler stuck on his head, and he wasn't working and they was paying him about fifty quid a month, whatever that is in dollars, so it was beer money but worth it, and most of the time it wasn't a problem cos he had to wear a hat any road cos it's cold up there in that bit of Canada int it? But there was this thunderstorm with lightning one night and the hail stones was big like golf balls and it had tekken out the roof of his barn where he kept his chickens and it was picking off the chickens one by one, with these big hail stones, and he loved his chickens more than anything in the world, so he just ran straight out in his pajamas without thinking, and the lightning spotted that flash of magnesium and BANG – pinned him to the yard like a stuck pig.

MARFLEET: Is that true?

WHITCHELL: No. I made it up. Well, all yours seem to have had spectacular deaths.

MARFLEET: (*Kissing WHITCHELL.*) Thank you. Why don't you sell this place?

WHITCHELL: Council are tekking me to court. It needs new guttering. I can afford the guttering, but not the scaffolding to put it up. Your lot, Labour. None of them have ever done a day's work in their lives.

MARFLEET: I could lend you the money. But, of course that would involve taking money from a woman.

WHITCHELL: You don't wanna get involved in this place.

MARFLEET: What about the bank manager?

WHITCHELL: He's like all bank managers. He'll lend you an umbrella when the sun's shining.

IZZY comes out of the loo.

TITS: What's he fucking about at?! Ring! Shoulda done it mesen. Not an easy thing to do you know Izzy, burn a cold store down. As soon as you get it going all the ice melts and puts the fire out. Ha, ha! Oh come on Izz!

IZZY: What's the insurance worth?

TITS: Five hundred thousand.

TITS opens the windows and stands in the draught.

EDDIE returns with a bag of chips and a pattie, and a quart of whisky. He sits on the sofa. IRENE joins him. He kisses her and offers her a chip.

IRENE: I'll just have a chip.

EDDIE: What is it with firemen eh? I'm just walking back with the bag of chips and there's three of them there. You know how they do, just standing there, nowt to do. What they looking at. I mean, am I on fire? We're paying them to sit around all day growing moustaches.

IRENE: Yer mad you.

EDDIE: Eh Irene, worrabout this, the bloke in the chippie had an eye patch. And a limp.

IRENE: (*She knows.*) What was the chippie called?

EDDIE: Treasure Island. Ah! That'll be it then. That's not a bad idea actually. An eye patch and a limp. I mean, for me.

IRENE: You're not thinking of gerrin a limp back are yer?

EDDIE: A limp, an eye patch, and yer own catchphrase. That'd work.

IRENE: An eye patch, a limp, yer own catchphrase and every now and then falling in dock –

EDDIE: Na! They might think there's summat wrong with me. It's a fine line.

IRENE: I saw a woman on Thursday in Hammonds. She looked just like I want to look when I'm old. She was about thirty. She had a long kind of caramel coloured coat on and shoes with kitten heels, and her hair straight, but curled at the ends. She was tall and happy, but happy's not all the story, she was confident.

EDDIE: Was she posh?

IRENE: She dunt work on fish dock.

EDDIE: She might have had the day off. Got dressed up.

IRENE: You can't dress away fish dock.

EDDIE: I'll get you them clothes. Hammonds was it?

IRENE: She didn't get them clothes in Hammonds, or anywhere in Hull. London, Paris mebbe.

EDDIE: I bin to London you know. It's overpriced. Guess how much half a kit of North Sea codling was? Four quid.

IRENE: You're serious about this fish merchant thing aren't yer?

EDDIE: How many fish trains are there every day from Hull? Go on guess.

IRENE: Seven hundred and twenty five.

EDDIE: Eight. But there used to be ten. Jesus Christ on a Raft uncle Ted ses by next year there'll be onny two. Cadora – they've already got vans. But! This is it! They go out full of fish, and d'yer know what, go on, guess!

IRENE: Just tell me!

EDDIE: They come back empty. Now, d'yer remember that lesson Bullet Head give us on the slave trade?

IRENE: Danny Elder claimed to be African cos his dad come from Bristol.

EDDIE: Yeah, it was pots and pans to Africa, slaves to America, and cotton back to Bristol. Them ships was never empty! Brilliant!

IRENE: Typical you that is. Thinking the slave trade's brilliant.

He stands. He's excited now and animated.

EDDIE: If a van goes to Warwick, farming int it? Fish out, meat back. There's twelve trawlers goes on the tide every day each with twenty blokes staying out for three weeks. That's a fuck of a lot of hot dinners Irene.

IRENE: Don't swear.

EDDIE: I'm excited! Me own triangular trade! I can make it work Irene, for us. Where d'yer wanna live Irene?

IRENE: Kirkella.

EDDIE: Kirkella!? Fuck! Alright. Kirkella it is.

IRENE: The meat'll smell of fish.

EDDIE: Oh, that's that then. The whole plan's scuppered.

They laugh and kiss.

IRENE: How's me dad gonna pay for all this?

EDDIE: Tick.

IRENE: He won't have owt to do with that tick man. I'm worried. He an't got this sort of money.

EDDIE: He'll do a trip a Christmas trip.

IRENE: Christmas cracker crew?

EDDIE: (*Laughing.*) Aye, he's right there!

IRENE: He's never done one of them trips.

EDDIE: He could get hissen med up to third hand, or winchman. Better money. It'll be a step up for him.

IRENE: He don't want a step up!

EDDIE: Everybody wants a step up.

IRENE: He's not like that!

EDDIE: It's an opportunity. At Christmas yer mate goes up to skipper, thirdhand goes up to mate, what's yer dad,

deckhand, he could go up to third hand or winchman.
The mate's the onny one yer have to worry about.

IRENE: How d'yer mean?

EDDIE: Chance to prove hissen, you know as a skipper.
They're mad for it. Fish in bad weather, cut allsorts of
corners, that's how they get the name innit, Christmas
cracker crew. Fucking barmy.

IRENE: I'm not having him doing that, not for me, just to
pay for a bit of luxury.

EDDIE: (*Angry.*) What the fuck do you want?! That none of
us ever have owt like this?! We could've had reception in
Andrews and gone to me Uncle Ted's caravan in
Reighton Gap, but oh no, that's not good enough for you
is it?!

IRENE: I'm not listening.

IRENE turns to her book.

EDDIE: Stop bloody worrying about summat that an't
happened, and in't gonna happen!

IZZY: Close the window. It's cold in here.

TITS: Cawld? It's like a bloody Turkish bathhouse in here.
Always was.

TITS feels the radiators.

If I buy this place that's the first thing I'll do.
Accidentally bust the thermostat.

TITS closes the window.

There you go. I've closed it. Happy now?

IZZY: (*With deep sarcasm.*) Happy.

EDDIE: It's hot in here. Can I open a window?

IRENE: I don't want anyone seeing in.

EDDIE: To look in from out there you'd have to be drowning.

WHITCHELL: Can I open a window love?

MARFLEET: Tut! It's as cold as ever in here.

WHITCHELL: Rubbish.

MARFLEET: I hate this room.

TITS: Cawld. Ice. I'd be nowt without it. You don't know what I've been through.

IRENE: It's cold in here.

EDDIE: D'yer know what we do down in the fish room, when you can't feel yer hands no more?

IRENE: I don't want to know!

EDDIE: I won't tell yer then. Anyhow, you wouldn't believe it.

TITS: I had to piss on my hands every day.

IZZY: I'm sick of listening to your suffering! It's taught you nowt but cruelty! You're a cartoon. They call you 'Tits'! A name you invented for yourself. Chose!

TITS: (*Aggressive.*) You wanna try working in the fish room. It's a lot different from mekking a visit.

IZZY: You said that to hurt me!

TITS: It's you bottling it up for twenty-five years, what's turned it into a big thing. Talk about it! Get it out yer system!

IZZY: I'm never gonna tell you what I saw down there.

TITS: I can guess. I know worr 'appened to him. He shoulda paid for this room on tick. I said that at the time.

IZZY: You're wicked!

TITS: The truth's always fucking wicked.

WHITCHELL: I bought this hotel, for him.

MARFLEET: You bought it for yourself.

WHITCHELL: To honour him.

MARFLEET: That's for yourself.

WHITCHELL: Clever. Why was it you who went down dock? Why din't yer mam go?

MARFLEET: They wouldn't let her. They were worried about what she might do.

WHITCHELL: Yeah, but she din't know about the… you know… the nature of the accident did she?

MARFLEET: No, they hadn't told anyone about that. I was the first to see the –

WHITCHELL: – I know that.

TITS: Did they have him laid out on the ice? Love?

IZZY: I'm never gonna tell yer.

MARFLEET: They'd tried to sort of put his head back on the end of the body, like put him back together again, but the ice had melted and there was a gap, you know, at the neck.

TITS: He weren't the first man to lose his head in the winch. Not the last either. Ten year back Sid Greening got guillotined an'all, mind you that was the messenger wire, not the winch. Christmas cracker crew again.

MARFLEET: They'd tried to dignify him by boxing the body in with wood, like a coffin. Four boards. Each one had Dux written on it. What is that Eddie? D U X.

WHITCHELL: Dux? Haddock. HadDUX.

MARFLEET: 'Course.

IZZY: His face –

TITS: – Alright, alright, I don't wanna know. Izzy please! You'll upset yersen.

IZZY: It was a boy's face. Like a kid who'd fallen off his bike, or stood on a nail. A scowl, not much more. Boyish. His teeth, bad; his hair, stiff with the ice.

TITS: I wanna buy this hotel – to honour him.

IZZY: He's already paid for this room.

TITS: Exactly! It's his room.

IZZY: Sentimental!

EDDIE: What yer reading?

IRENE: I'm not reading.

MARFLEET: Are you going to write a suicide note then?

WHITCHELL: Er… na. Never been one for writing. I'm a telephone man me. I'll ring everyone up. I don't want to tempt them into having an inquiry.

MARFLEET: Quite enjoyable inquiries. That's how I started.

WHITCHELL: Aye.

MARFLEET: I felt a bit guilty actually, you know, for enjoying it so much. It was the first time I'd ever seen any formal attempt at any kind of justice. Two weeks, I didn't miss a second. Barristers, solicitors –

WHITCHELL: – Bastards.

MARFLEET: – Lord… kaw! I've forgotten his name. The way they talked.

WHITCHELL: Professional liars all of them.

MARFLEET: The words they used to describe the accident. 'Mr Wilson was an ingénue winchman.' (*Laughing.*) Ridiculous. An ingénue winchman.

WHITCHELL: What the fuck does that mean?

MARFLEET: Inexperienced.

WHITCHELL: Why din't he just say that then?

MARFLEET: She. 'In a turbulent sea a splint in the wire snagged in his oil frock and he was carried inexorably…', 'inexorably', 'towards the drum of the winch.' You can't beat that death Eddie, so why try?

WHITCHELL: It's not a competition.

MARFLEET: You know better than anyone that I made a point of never talking about going down dock that day, but one time I was stuck, we were stuck, in Belfast, the talks were going nowhere. I'd lost them a bit, I needed to re-assert some sort of personal legitimacy. They'd all lived with death and revenge and all the awfulness of the Troubles for years, and who was I, another Brit, another minister, another big warm-hearted woman, well they could see straight through that for what it was. So I told both sides, separate rooms of course, proximity talks, told them both about when I was eighteen, going down dock, climbing them steps down into the fishroom and seeing my father's body on the ice with the head next to it. The next day we managed to get six of them, three and three, in a room together, the same bloody room for once. Well, the rest is history. I still feel dirty about it. Like I've used him. We don't need another death Eddie. How old are you?

WHITCHELL: Same age as you, always have been.

MARFLEET: Sixty-seven. You might live another thirty years.

WHITCHELL: That's what I don't want.

EDDIE: Stop reading will yer! You're not reading. I know you, you're worrying, worrying about summat that hasn't even happened.

EDDIE: Can't you just accept the gift?! He wants to give you a taste of something better. He might get summat out of it. He might like been third hand, or winchman. More money in his pocket, bit of respect, authority. Aye, it might be the beginning of summat for him.

IRENE: Don't talk about my dad like that!

EDDIE pulls the book out of her hand and throws it aside.

EDDIE: (*With growing anger.*) You don't understand do you? He's trying to give you summat the only way he can, by working, by gutting fucking fish. He's gonna give up his Christmas so we can have this, you can have this, this bloody fairy castle for his precious princess. And I want the same for yer, but I'm different, I'm not gonna gut fish, I'm not gonna give them bastards my life. I'm not saying yer dad's not a good man, but I've got summat else, I've got a fight in me, I learnt it in them swimming baths down Albert Ave, I can do anything, I've proven it to mesen. I'll get yer inside a big Kirkella house. Carpets, warm. But I'll do it my way, not yer dad's way, and it won't involve reading books neither. Aye, it won't be pretty, and it won't be polite but sooner or later I'm gonna fucking kick my way in!

IRENE: Can I have me book back please?

EDDIE: Yeah, sorry.

He collects the book.

(*Pronounced with a sharp A.*) 'The Grapes of Wrath.'

IRENE: Wrath not wrath. (*Phonetically = wroth not wrath.*)

EDDIE stands, separate from her, and lights a cigarette, and paces round the room.

TITS: Yer mam shoulda gone. You'd go if it were me. It'll be burning now. Should go up alright. Wooden roof int it. What time is it!? Why dun't he bloody ring!? What we gonna do Izz?

IZZY: I want to go to university.

TITS: Eh? Bloody hell, you're forty-three.

IZZY: I've got a place at Manchester.

TITS: How come I don't know anything about this?

IZZY: I'm telling you now. A law degree.

TITS: What's wrong with Hull? I've heard it's a good university.

Where's whatshisname fit into all this?

IZZY: (*Correcting him.*) Martin. I'm going to end it. It's not love.

TITS: I'm too thick. I don't get it.

IZZY: I'll come home every Easter, summer and Christmas.

TITS: Aye, well we know all about that caper don't we. Will you be bringing a different dyke girlfriend home every time an'all? When I think of what went on in that spare room of ours. Waste of money decorating. I don't see how we can go from Strickie Ave, setting up the business, having Harriet, fuck knows how many miscarriages –

IZZY: Three.

TITS: Three? Bloody hell. Feels like ten. National Ave, Cott Road, Willerby, Kirkella. Is it… do we end here? I'd like to pay for you to go to school.

IZZY: University!

TITS: There must be fees aren't there? And living money. You're not eighteen, you can't live on jam sandwiches. And you can come home if you want, and don't if you don't. That would give me pleasure.

IZZY: You don't have any money.

TITS is heavily defeated. The phone rings. He picks it up.

(*On the phone.*) Tits… yeah… good… I'm gonna put the phone down now Francis, well done, I'm pleased with yer… don't forget, go to the police in the morning. Night, night.

TITS puts the phone down. And lights a cigar, and goes to stand on the balcony.

I've got money coming.

MARFLEET: How are you going to kill yourself?

WHITCHELL: Gonna hang mesen at the pictures. Men in Black Two.

MARFLEET: You never ever went to the cinema.

WHITCHELL: I know. It'll be a nice change for me.

MARFLEET: I thought you'd choose fire.

WHITCHELL: Aye, fire. Fire or ice. That's been my life. Don't fancy fire. Hot innit. Ice. Cawld.

MARFLEET: You like the cold. Look! You are joking aren't you Eddie? Please love. This is… it's not funny!

WHITCHELL: I like a cold sea.

MARFLEET: You still swim then?

WHITCHELL: In the sea. You float easier, the salt is like a hand. Old Father Neptune looks after you. Yeah, he can give as well as take. You didn't know that did you? I swam to Scarborough yesterday.

MARFLEET: What? Round Flamborough Head? That's twenty miles.

WHITCHELL: I got the bus back. I get some funny looks. It's the goose grease I think, or the trunks. I go out the door, left at the florists, through Woollies, out the back, over the prom, and down onto the beach. Straight in, no messing. Swim round Flamborough. Get out at South Bay, over the road to the bus terminus, and back here.

MARFLEET: Where do you keep your bus pass?

WHITCHELL: They know me.

MARFLEET: It'll upset people. Hanging yourself in a cinema.

WHITCHELL: That was a joke. My preference would be for a controlled explosion. You know, total disintegration. But I think that's a bit beyond me skill level.

The phone rings. This brings TITS in from the balcony. IZZY stands. TITS picks up the phone.

TITS: (*On the phone.*) Tits. Eh?… Eddie Whitchell… yeah, Blue Triangle Distribution. Who are you?… Have you put it out?… Arson!?… there's petrol on site for the fork lifts… A dead body?… Y E B?… His name's Yebsley, Ian Calvert, lives down Wheeler Street… I sacked him last year… I'm on me silver wedding… Jackie's there is he, good… he's my production manager, yeah he'll secure the site… thanks.

He puts the phone down and sinks onto the bed. He is genuinely shaken.

(*Increasingly inarticulate ending up in sobs.*) Yebsley. He must've gone back for more, and Francis dint see him the second time. Agh. He's dead. Oh God. Overcome by smoke. He was only a kid, a kid. Bit of a rum un but... oh Jesus. No. Oh no. Oh God, Izzy, the kid's dead. He's dead. He's dead. Oh no. He's dead.

IZZY sits with him and holds him, his head buried in her shoulder. He cries.

IZZY: Come on Eddie. Come on!

TITS: I'm sorry Izz. I've let you down. The kid's dead. It'll be murder. Will it? Izzy?!

IZZY: How can it be murder?

TITS: What's the other one they have?

IZZY: Manslaughter.

TITS: That's it! The kid's dead.

IZZY: What have you arranged with Francis?

TITS: He burns it down and then he goes down the copshop and admits to doing it. I'll go down for this!

IZZY: When will Francis go to the police?

TITS: I dunno, I dunno.

IZZY: You've got to talk to Francis. Tell him not to go to the police.

TITS: How does that help?

IZZY: What's the matter with you?! Look, I don't believe it, you can't see it can you? It's there staring you in the face and you can't see it.

TITS: What?

IZZY: Yebsley. They'll think Yebsley started the fire.

TITS: Bloody hell! You're right. A grudge. For laying him off. Jesus.

IZZY: Ring Francis.

TITS: I don't believe you thought of that. That that's your idea.

IZZY: It's not my idea. It's obvious. It's what you would think of if you weren't panicking. It's your idea. I'm telling you what your idea is.

TITS: Ring Francis. If only it was that easy. He's a vagrant! They're not on the fucking phone are they!

IZZY: Where's he stay?

TITS: That hostel, what is it Great Passage Street.

IZZY picks up the phone and dials the reception desk.

IZZY: (*On the phone.*) Do you have a Hull directory there please?… the William Booth hostel, Great Passage Street… Thank you.

TITS: Look at yer. Fucking brilliant. I'm nothing without you Izz. Look at yer.

IZZY: This is your idea. I feel dirty.

TITS: I'm sorry. Everything I fucking touch I –

IZZY: – shutup! (*On the phone.*) Yeah, 770652. Thank you… and I'd like an outside line please… thanks.

She dials and gives the phone to TITS.

TITS: Hello… I need to talk to Francis Wiles… yeah, I know, this is important, is he there?… How drunk is he?.Can you go and get him please. It's important… I'm from the *Hull Daily Mail*, he's won Spot the Ball… Thank you.

TITS waits on the phone. IRENE stands and goes over to EDDIE. She undoes the buttons on his shirt.

EDDIE: You know when I went down to Billingsgate, on that reckie?

IRENE: Yeah.

EDDIE: There was this cockney dealer. 'Facking 'ell china, at the end of the day you gotta give it to him ainch ya, fack, fack, fack.' Ha! He walked past everyone and he said the same thing. 'Gimme the tits!' Sometimes he'd say 'Gimme the tits, I don't want the arse!' You know, like what he was saying was I want the best fish, don't pass me off with any reds or dogs or owt. 'Gimme the tits!' What do you think?

IRENE: What do I think? About what?

EDDIE: 'Gimme the tits'. For me catchphrase.

IRENE: I think it's crude, and ugly.

EDDIE: It's funny though int it?

IRENE: (*Angry.*) Do you want people to laugh at you then?! Do you want to be a joke?!

EDDIE: (*Not listening, excited.*) They'd shorten it to 'Gimme'. That's not bad. 'Gimme.' Sounds a bit Jewish! That's good for a merchant.

IRENE: You're alright! As you are! You're beautiful Eddie, you're brilliant! I love you! Will you just stop being so bloody stupid!

EDDIE: You don't swear. Beautiful? Am I? God.

IRENE: Yes.

IRENE takes off her dress, revealing rather elaborate white lingerie, and a slip. She's embarrassed. EDDIE watches, getting interested. She then takes off the slip, and just stands there. EDDIE gawps.

EDDIE: Kaw! You look fanbloodytastic Irene.

IRENE: (*Referring to the lingerie.*) It's better than black isn't it? Suits my colouring don't you think?

EDDIE: Yeah. You know that nurse's uniform you had when you were a kid?

IRENE: Yeah.

EDDIE: Have you still got it?

IRENE: Why?

EDDIE: Just asking.

EDDIE takes his shirt off revealing the very fresh tattoo of a panther's head.

IRENE: (*At the panther's head.*) What's that?

EDDIE: A panther's head. Do you like it?

IRENE: Couldn't you have had summat different?

EDDIE: Like what? A panther's arse?

IRENE: Oh shurrup.

EDDIE: (*Referring to the lingerie.*) Where did you get this stuff?

IRENE: Hammonds. Dad give us some money. I told him I bought a pressure cooker.

EDDIE: You did the right thing. I'll gerra pressure cooker for yer.

IRENE: Make love to me. Please Eddie.

EDDIE: Aye, why not.

They kiss. They start getting carried away, and head towards the bed.

TITS: (*On the phone.*) Francis?!… Now listen carefully. What you don't know is that Yebsley came back for a second bite… yeah, and he's dead now… yeah, dead, smoke inhalation… yeah. So you, are you listening, stop that, stop that, and fucking listen, you…

(*To IZZY.*) He's flipped.

(*On the phone.*) Listen!! Stop fucking blubbing! You don't say owt to anybody, alright? Do not go to the police. Do not admit doing it. I'll sort you out Francis… You don't have to go to prison this way… Because Yebsley's gonna get the blame. You talk to no-one. Understand?… Good. Tarra. Just act normal!

Phone down.

How does a fucking alcoholic vagrant with a three legged dog act normal?

MARFLEET comes out of the bathroom. She dresses, and takes her coat from the wardrobe. MARFLEET and WHITCHELL kiss, a goodbye kiss. She turns and heads towards the door.

MARFLEET: I hate this room. I'm going to go now.

WHITCHELL: We got a lot done.

MARFLEET: I'll get my solicitor to write. He'll send –

WHITCHELL: – mek yer plans, I'll not be an obstacle.

MARFLEET: I don't have any doubt that you will kill yourself. Tell me what I do now Eddie.

WHITCHELL: You turn round, put your coat on, give us a squeeze, and fuck off back to Belgium.

MARFLEET: What if I call the police? An ambulance? I could save your life, get you sectioned. But you always get what you want. Something happened to me Eddie.

WHITCHELL: Aye, you became someone else.

MARFLEET: You've changed. This asceticism of yours, does that mean that you believe in something?

WHITCHELL: Reincarnation.

MARFLEET: And what do you want to come back as?

WHITCHELL: A panda. Or Pele.

MARFLEET: I've met Pele. I liked him. He made me laugh.

WHITCHELL: That's because he's me.

She laughs.

MARFLEET: I met a baker recently in Paris, Jean-Claude Dubur. Brussels, the European Parliament, are going to close him down, which is why I went to meet him.

WHITCHELL: Why are we talking about bakers?

MARFLEET: Shutup and listen cos this might be the last thing you ever hear me say.

WHITCHELL: You've become a right hard nut, an't yer.

MARFLEET: I try.

During the next she begins to weep, not sobs, but tears.

The flour he uses is in contravention of at least seven food safety statutes. Which is why they're going to close him down. His great, great, great, great, great grandfather used to sell bread to the crowds that came to watch the guillotine. Jean-Claude hasn't changed the basic recipe, and the bread is beautiful, quite beautiful. They fly an order to Colonel Gadaffi in Libya every day. Salvador Dali asked him to make a picture frame out of bread. That's what got him started. So he made sculptures out of bread, the chair you sit on when you order is made out of bread. Last year he made a birdcage, out of bread, and put a bird in it, and people came and watched the bird eat its way out, and then fly away.

WHITCHELL: Why are you telling me this?

She recovers.

MARFLEET: He killed himself last week.

WHITCHELL: What's wrong wi' bin a baker? Why's he wanna be a bloody artist? Typical of the modern world. Every second milkman you meet nowadays is writing a novel, or trying to be an actor, or summat else equally flakey, as if delivering the milk int good enough for them. They end up delivering the milk badly.

MARFLEET: How do you deliver milk badly?

WHITCHELL: With a grudge. When hauling water, just haul water. Confucius.

They hug.

(*Handing it over.*) You'll need the key. Post it through the letterbox. Don't forget. I don't want to be locked in.

She heads for the door, opens it, looks at him, and then the room. She is now bigger and stronger than the room and looks it in the eye. Then she moves off and closes the door behind her.

TITS: That's that then. Bloody hell. We've gorr away with it.

(*Beat.*) He was robbing the place. I mean if yer go out robbing yer taking yer life in yer hands aren't yer.

(*Beat.*) D'yer fancy a swim Izz? I wanna swim. I can only think clearly when I'm swimming. Did yer pack me trunks?

EDDIE and IRENE are kissing on the bed.

IRENE: I want you to wear two johnnies.

He stops his kissing and flops as if defeated yet again.

Just to be sure. Please.

EDDIE: Two!? What? One on me head and –

IRENE: – don't mek a joke out of it Eddie. Please. You know, to be sure, like. I don't want to get pregnant. Not before I'm twennie at least.

EDDIE: (*With a sigh.*) Two, eh?

IRENE: Please.

EDDIE starts putting on the condoms.

WHITCHELL: (*On the phone.*) Good evening young man… Yes, you can help, I just rang to say I don't have a television licence… I've never had one, no… Er.nineteen fifty eight… forty six years, kaw! Is that a record?… colour… no, no, no, you don't understand, I don't want a licence… I just rang up to tell you that I haven't got one… no, I'm not going to tell you where I live cos that would spoil the fun wunt it… alright, I'll give yer a clue, NEAR Pitlochry… Scotland, yeah, will you send one of them vans?… Fair enough, I'm gonna go now cos there's one of them car chase video programmes on, and I like them, I prefer the British ones… the American ones are alright, but I think they use actors… I'll leave you to it… Yes, Pitlochry, tarra.

WHITCHELL goes to a drawer and takes out his trunks. He strips off, and puts his trunks on. He then goes back to the drawer and takes out a pot of goose grease. He greases his whole body with it. He puts on a bathing cap, and a pair of goggles, which he puts on, tests, and then lets sit on the top of his head. From the drawer he takes a pair of flippers. He doesn't put these on but walks to the door opens it leaving the flippers on the floor in the hallway. He heads off down the corridor leaving the door open.

EDDIE has put on the condoms.

EDDIE: You're happy enough with two are yer?

IRENE: (*Checking.*) I'm sorry Eddie, it's just…

EDDIE: Alright, alright, don't go on about it.

He joins IRENE between the sheets. He moves on top of her and they kiss.

IRENE: Try not to hurt me Eddie.

EDDIE: It dunt hurt. I've told you.

He penetrates her. IRENE makes a noise and stops his movement.

Did that hurt?

IRENE: Yes. But it was a nice hurt. Don't stop.

She makes a second cry.

TITS: It's gonna be alright I think Izz.

TITS goes over to IZZY and holds her. She holds him.

IZZY: There's cats on my curtains.

TITS: There's dogs on my wall. Quiet int it. I'm going to put in an offer on this place, Izz.

EDDIE and IRENE make love and give off gentle, and sporadic noises. It is not experienced or skilful love making.

WHITCHELL returns with a big jerry can of petrol. He douses the whole room with petrol from the can, including the bed, IRENE and EDDIE, and the bathroom. Then he stands in the doorway and surveys the room. He lights a match and immediately the lights go to black.

To black and

The End.